"Tom Bunn uses his decades of flying experience and advanced education in clinical social work to provide an all-encompassing approach to panic. Bunn's holistic approach precisely addresses the biological factors involved in the panic response and provides tools to regulate the intensity of feelings and overcome their effects. This is a must-read!"

— **Donald Arthur, MD,** vice admiral, US Navy (retired), and 35th Navy surgeon general

"A treasured gift for sufferers of anxiety and panic, with detailed techniques supported by proven science, *Panic Free* takes readers by the hand to help them successfully triumph over feelings of anxiety and panic."

— **Athena Carr,** school psychologist

"Tom Bunn's program is remarkably effective and liberates anyone suffering with panic and anxiety. His versatile ten-day program is anchored in physiological and psychological research and can be applied to any of life's panic- and anxiety-inducing events."

— **Walter A. Figiel, MBA,** SOAR program graduate

"I am both a fearful flyer and a practicing psychotherapist, and I have found *Panic Free* to be extremely helpful in both arenas. As a psychotherapist, I recommend the book for my patients with anxiety of any kind, and we practice the techniques during therapy sessions with highly effective results. I especially appreciate that *Panic Free* is based on the latest brain research and understanding of how the human mind works. My patients and I both thank you, Tom Bunn!"

— **David Lundin, MA, LLP, LPC**

"Thanks to Tom Bunn's teaching, I can control my panic anxiety without medication for the first time.... Bunn's clear and vivid explanation of how our brains, hormones, and conditioning

create panic and how we can use vagal braking to control panic provides clear steps for positive change."
— **Morra Aarons-Mele,** author of *Hiding in the Bathroom* and founder of Women Online

"Allows everyone to embrace their full potential with specific, focused, clearly explained, and practical steps to break free from panic attacks. Hurry, buy the book and transform your life."
— **Marla Friedman, PsyD, PC,** licensed psychologist and Badge of Life board chairman

"Provides a method for overcoming even extreme anxiety that works. I know from personal experience."
— **Carole,** whose story about going through tunnels is included in *Panic Free*

"Captain Tom's unique capacity to use clinical examples and simple analogies allows him to render even the most complex neuroscientific information in a way that is both comprehensible and fun to read."
— **Judith Pearson, PhD,** director, International Masterson Institute

"A reader-friendly guide to becoming anxiety free using an innovative, scientifically sound, and experience-tested method. Moreover, this approach is very simple to implement. I have used this technique both in my clinical practice and personally, and found it very useful and effective. Anyone who is suffering from anxiety should read this book."
— **Olga Savina, PhD,** psychotherapist

"Through Captain Tom's fear-of-flying program, I was able to overcome my phobia of flying, which I had for forty-one years. Captain Tom's book *Panic Free* expands upon his proven technique to help others with a variety of anxiety-producing fears and panic."
— **Wanda Dougherty,** SOAR program graduate

PANIC
FREE

Also by Tom Bunn

SOAR: The Breakthrough Treatment for Fear of Flying

PANIC FREE

*The 10-Day Program to End
Panic, Anxiety, and Claustrophobia*

TOM BUNN, LCSW

Afterword by Stephen W. Porges, PhD

New World Library
Novato, California

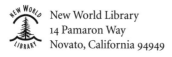

New World Library
14 Pamaron Way
Novato, California 94949

Text design by Tona Pearce Myers

Library of Congress Cataloging-in-Publication Data

Names: Bunn, Tom, author.
Title: Panic free : the ten-day program to end panic, anxiety, and claustrophobia / Tom Bunn, LCSW.
Description: Novato, California : New World Library, [2019] | Includes bibliographical references and index.
Identifiers: LCCN 2018046216 (print) | LCCN 2018046739 (ebook) | ISBN 9781608686063 (ebook) | ISBN 9781608686056 (print : alk. paper)
Subjects: LCSH: Panic disorders--Popular works. | Panic disorders--Treatment.
Classification: LCC RC535 (ebook) | LCC RC535 .B86 2019 (print) | DDC 616.85/223--dc23
LC record available at https://lccn.loc.gov/2018046216

First printing, April 2019
ISBN 978-1-60868-605-6
Ebook ISBN 978-1-60868-606-3
Printed in the United States on 50% postconsumer-waste recycled paper

 New World Library is proud to be a Gold Certified Environmentally Responsible Publisher. Publisher certification awarded by Green Press Initiative.

10   9   8   7   6   5   4   3

*To the many panic sufferers who,
despite expecting that nothing would work,
had the courage to try one more time*

Contents

Part IV. Your Ten-Day Plan to End Panic and Claustrophobia Forever

Part I

Your Introduction to Automatic Control

CHAPTER 1

A Future Free of Panic and Claustrophobia

If you have struggled with panic and found no relief, I know the frustration. As an airline pilot, I tried for years to help fearful fliers control panic, using every known method. Nothing worked.

After years of experimentation, I stumbled on a solution. Since then, every client who has learned this new way to manage anxiety has been able to control panic when flying. Though our principal aim was to control panic in the air, clients reported an unexpected benefit: they were free from panic on the ground as well. This approach changed their lives. It can change yours, too. This book can lead you to a future free from panic and claustrophobia.

This breakthrough, like many important discoveries, took place accidentally after years of searching for a solution. The search began in 1980 at Pan Am, where I was a pilot and volunteered to help with the airline's fear-of-flying course. The pilot who led the course told participants they could conquer their fear of flying by letting go of control and by using breathing exercises to stay relaxed. The course ended with a "graduation flight." Some participants got through the flight all right, but others panicked despite diligently performing their breathing exercises. The pilot in charge believed his advice was adequate. Unable to fault them on their breathing exercises, he told them, "You didn't let go."

Panic is an awful experience. Being blamed by people who don't understand makes it worse. It was distressing to watch this scenario play out in course after course. The suffering — and my powerlessness to relieve it — set me on a quest. I set up a fear-of-flying course of my own, called SOAR. It included every known technique for combating panic. Some techniques came from mental health professionals; some came from panic sufferers. Each technique was helpful to some people in some ways. But all these techniques put together still weren't enough to help every participant control panic.

The search continued. I went to graduate school, became a licensed therapist, and attended one postgraduate training institute after another. I studied Gestalt therapy, neuro-linguistic programming, psychodynamic psychotherapy, Ericksonian hypnosis, and cognitive behavioral therapy. Again, various aspects of these therapies helped some clients, but not all.

Cognitive behavioral therapy (CBT) was a new and seemingly promising approach. It is based on the idea that what we feel is caused by what we think. Therefore, to control our feelings, we must learn to control our thoughts. I developed new CBT-based techniques for clients to use on their flights. These new tools worked for some clients, but they did not work for those whose panic developed rapidly. For them, the slightest movement of the plane was like a spark that quickly turned into a wildfire. Emotion instantly overcame them. Even while using the breathing techniques I had taught them, they went straight into full-blown panic.

Looking back, there are two obvious reasons why CBT could not help these clients. First, though it's true that panic can be caused by thoughts, it can also erupt with no conscious thought at all. Second, whether panic is triggered consciously or unconsciously, the real issue is something else: inability to regulate the intensity of feelings. Normally, intensity is regulated by unconscious processes. If these processes fail, imaginary threats can escalate quickly into the belief that life-threatening dangers exist. If escape is not immediately at hand, a person feels trapped, and panic results. CBT did not address the lack of unconscious regulation.

We can think of regulation as working like the thermostat in a home, which is supposed to keep the ambient temperature in a comfortable range. The thermostat does this job without our needing to think about it. We may not know how it works, but we know it isn't working right if the room temperature soars to one hundred degrees. Similarly, your emotional thermostat is supposed to work without your needing to think about it. When you panic, something has gone wrong with that thermostat.

Which takes us back to the snag with cognitive behavioral therapy. Cognition is a conscious process, but the regulation of arousal — arousal being how revved up we are — is an unconscious process. CBT does not engage the unconscious part of the brain where regulation of arousal should take place. You probably know the old joke about the drunk looking for his keys. Though he lost them elsewhere, he's looking for them under a lamppost because "that's where the light is." Unfortunately, when looking for the keys to unlock panic, I was like the drunk. I was looking not where the action was — where the processes of arousal regulation were taking place — but where the conscious processes were observable. It didn't work. To find a solution to panic, I had to do what the drunk needed to do: leave the lamppost and grope around in the dark. I needed to stop looking at processes I could observe and start finding ways to understand and manage processes I couldn't observe.

If a technique could be devised to control panic, it would have to work the way regulation is supposed to work: automatically and unconsciously. Once panic starts to develop, what a person does consciously — which is to say, cognitively — is unlikely to help. If we believe something life-threatening is happening, and there is no possible way to escape it, we panic. If, however, we can examine our thinking and see that the life-threatening thing is not actually happening, we won't panic. CBT trains people to stop and examine their thinking. If they can do that, they can prevent panic. But in a state of near panic, most people are simply incapable of rational thought. Under stress, imagination takes over, and a situation that is not life-threatening is experienced as life-threatening. That is the first factor that causes panic. The second is the conviction that this situation, truly believed to be life-threatening, cannot be escaped. The person's cognitive abilities desert them. As a client told me, "If you asked my name, I couldn't tell you." Someone in this state can't examine what is going on in their mind skillfully enough to recognize its inaccuracy.

The therapist Jerilyn Ross was also looking for a way to

help clients control panic that did not rely on cognition. She came up with a technique she called "thought stopping." She instructed clients to wear a rubber band on one wrist and to snap it every time an anxiety-provoking thought entered their mind. She believed that the association of pain with the anxiety-provoking thoughts would inhibit the thoughts and keep them from causing panic.

Though this reasoning made sense, the idea of self-inflicted pain didn't sit well with me. Instead of thought stopping, I tried thought redirection. I trained my fear-of-flying clients to bring a positive memory to mind each time an anxiety-provoking thought arose. For example, I taught an athlete to automatically shift anxious thoughts about flying to her memory of running the New York marathon. In her case, thought redirection worked. I taught a young man to redirect thoughts of flying to the moment he proposed to his wife. He did fine. So did several clients who redirected thoughts of flying to memories of making their wedding vows. But overall, the results were hit or miss. For some clients, this technique was helpful. For others, it did nothing at all.

One day, I was teaching thought redirection to a new client, the mother of a small baby. I asked her to name a powerful, positive experience she could use to shift her anxiety-producing thoughts. She said, "Nursing my baby." I thought to myself, "You've got to be crazy. You're going to get on the plane and think you'll never see your child again." Fortunately, I kept my thoughts to myself and went along with her idea. To my amazement, when she reported back, she said the flight had gone perfectly. She did not experience a single ripple of anxiety!

In the months that followed, a few more mothers chose to redirect anxiety-producing thoughts to nursing. They, too, reported complete success. Had we stumbled on a key to the problem? If so, what was it? Why did a memory of nursing a baby work better than a memory of running a marathon, scoring the winning goal, or graduating from college?

It soon became clear that these exceptional results were not due to thought redirection. Research by Sue Carter, Kerstin Uvnäs Moberg, and others has found that mothers produce oxytocin during nursing, and that oxytocin inhibits the release of the stress hormones that give rise to feelings of fear, claustrophobia, and panic. When my clients redirected their thoughts from their fear of flying to their memories of nursing, flying actually became associated with nursing, and being on the plane triggered the release of oxytocin, which blocked the stress hormones.

Nature inhibits the release of stress hormones to prioritize the child's needs for nourishment. Suppose a new mother is nursing her child when she gets a call that relatives are on the way over to see the new baby. The house is a mess. Will the relatives understand it is impossible to keep up with housework when there is a new baby? Or will they criticize her? If the mother becomes anxious about their visit, she might stop nursing and clean the house. The baby would not get proper nourishment. Nature takes care of that problem. Though things that need to be done come to mind, oxytocin prevents the release of stress hormones so that she feels no anxiety to stop nursing and prepare for the arrival of the relatives.

Since I stumbled on this discovery, I've been able to help several thousand formerly anxious fliers control panic by linking flying to one or more of the ways nature causes us to produce oxytocin. This is an amazing result, because no environment is more problematic for panic sufferers than being high above the earth, with no control of the situation and no means of escaping it. It's easy for them to persuade themselves that their fear is rational. After all, planes do crash. Turbulence can make a plane shake so hard that it may feel as though it's about to fall out of the sky.

This special panic-inducing environment became the lab in which my clients and I developed advanced methods to control panic. The oxytocin link was only the first discovery. I knew that redirecting thoughts about flying to memories of getting engaged or saying wedding vows could be effective in controlling anxiety, but why? It is because in these special moments, the brain and the body are signaled to override the effects of stress hormones. This gave us two ways to control fear, panic, and claustrophobia. The first prevents the release of stress hormones; the second overrides their effects. We will be exploring both methods in this book.

A bonus of this discovery was that as my clients succeeded at controlling their fear of flying, they also succeeded at controlling panic attacks on the ground — triggered by environments like bridges, tunnels, elevators, and MRI (magnetic resonance imaging) machines.

In parts 1 through 3 of this book, I first explain the physiological and psychological mechanisms that lead to panic. Then, in part 4, I lead you step by step through a ten-day program to establish automatic control of panic. In ten days, you can learn to put behind you the frustration, the worry, and the distress of panic and claustrophobia, in the air and on the ground.

Before You Start

Before embarking on the ten-day program, you must confirm that what you are dealing with really is panic and not an underlying medical condition.

Though symptoms of panic vary from person to person, the following symptoms are common:

- Palpitations, pounding heart, or accelerated heart rate
- Sweating
- Trembling or shaking
- Sensations of shortness of breath or suffocation
- Feelings of choking
- Chest pain or discomfort
- Nausea or abdominal distress
- Feeling dizzy, unsteady, light-headed, or faint
- Chills or hot flushes
- Numbness or tingling sensations (paresthesia)
- Feelings of unreality (derealization)
- Feelings of being detached from oneself (depersonalization)
- Fear of losing control or going crazy
- Fear of dying

Some of these symptoms, however, are also associated with other disorders. You need to discuss your symptoms with a physician to rule these out. And even if you have already talked them over with your doctor, it's a good idea to review your symptoms and any changes at your yearly physical examination.

CHAPTER 2

The Panic-Proof Part of Your Brain

Jan, an emergency room nurse, emailed the following:

In training, I was taught about dozens and dozens of situations. For everything that could happen, there was a plan. My instructor said, "If this happens, you do that, and if you see this going on, you have to fix it this way." The number of things I had to know how to react to was overwhelming. Even after we practiced responding to each situation again and again, I really doubted I could do the job. But I was surprised. Even the first day in the ER, what I had practiced kicked in.

You would think that a person who can operate as an ER nurse could handle anything. And, in general, I'm fine. But put me in a place where I can't get out, and I panic. I've done therapy to get rid of it, but nothing worked until I did this [the SOAR Fear of Flying Program].

It is said that first responders and emergency medical professionals do not "rise to the occasion" in life-and-death situations: rather, they "descend to the level of their training." Why? In life-threatening situations, the release of stress hormones can impede their high-level thinking. To function under extreme stress, they depend on a part of the brain that is immune to stress hormones: the unconscious procedural memory in the subcortex. In training, they repeatedly perform the various procedures they will need to carry out when under stress, installing every step of these procedures in this part of the brain so that they can perform them without having to depend on high-level thinking.

Though the concept of unconscious procedural memory may be new to you, if you are an experienced driver, you have been using it for years. You can drive and think of other things at the same time.

How did your unconscious procedural memory learn to drive a car? When you were a new driver, you focused your conscious mind (in the cerebral cortex) on the task. While you were doing this, your unconscious procedural memory (in the subcortex) was memorizing what you were doing. It learned to steer the car and keep the speed steady. Unconscious procedural memory can't make decisions, though. For example, it can't decide what freeway exit to take. If your mind is elsewhere as you near your exit, you may go right past it on "mental autopilot."

When you are alarmed or highly aroused, stress hormones are released, and your conscious mind, in the cortex, is overwhelmed. That is when panic can arise. But unconscious procedural memory, in the subcortex, is not bothered by stress hormones. Not only can it perform well-rehearsed mechanical tasks, but, if it is trained to do so, it can automatically activate your calming system, the parasympathetic nervous system.

In this ten-day program, you'll train your unconscious procedural memory to serve as your personal panic-controlling first responder. In the high-stress situations that now cause you to panic, it will step in and protect you.

Part II

Situational Control of Panic and Claustrophobia

CHAPTER 3

Carole's Holland Tunnel Challenge

Carole, a librarian, lives in Pennsylvania. After the attacks on September 11, 2001, she stopped driving to New York City through the Holland Tunnel, which enters Manhattan a few blocks north of the World Trade Center. The thought of being in the tunnel put her on the edge of panic. So she took a longer route, crossing the Hudson River by the George Washington Bridge. She told me she needed to pick up some friends at John F. Kennedy Airport. Going via the bridge instead of the tunnel would take an hour longer. Having already learned to control panic when flying, she wanted to know if she could train herself go through the tunnel without panic.

It was an easy call. If Carole could control her panic while flying, the tunnel would be a minor challenge. Though flying is remarkably safe, it frequently provokes panic. High above the earth, and especially at night or in clouds, passengers feel disconnected from the earth, the basis of their sense of control. In-flight turbulence can induce the fear that the plane might simply fall apart. Panic sends us the message to flee; but on a plane, there is no way to escape.

To make absolutely sure Carole's trip through the tunnel would be panic free, we did several things. The first was to establish links between the landmarks she would see on her trip and the memory of a calming event in the past. This meant that each landmark would have a calming effect when it came into view.

I asked Carole to make a list. "Start with what you see when you step out the door. Write that down. Then write down what you see when getting into your car, starting it, and going from your driveway into the street. List the landmarks you will see along the way." Her list included left turns, right turns, road signs, gas stations, the New Jersey Turnpike entrance. The list continued all the way to Kennedy Airport, and from there all the way back home. In addition to those familiar landmarks, it included moments Carole would find emotionally challenging, such as approaching the Holland Tunnel, entering it, and being a quarter of the way through it, halfway through it, and three-quarters of the way through it. We ended the exercise with the sensation of freedom: the thought of leaving the tunnel and driving in lower Manhattan.

Next, Carole associated each landmark with a calming memory. This memory doesn't have to be long or elaborate: it can be as simple as a recollection of being with a best friend. When you are with a friend who completely accepts you, you may feel your guard let down. When that happens, the parasympathetic branch of your nervous system — the part that calms your physiological responses — takes over and overrides the effects of any stress hormones in your system. Once Carole established links between the landmarks and a calming memory — hers was being with a friend who knew her struggles well — she was well on the way to automatically controlling her anxiety during the trip.

How did her trip work out? Carole reported that when she first saw the Holland Tunnel, she got a jolt of stress hormones. But because she had already worked to associate the tunnel with the memory of a calming person, the effects of the stress hormones quickly abated. She continued through the tunnel without difficulty. After picking up her friends at the airport, she came back through the tunnel. Then she encountered the situation she had dreaded. "I got stuck in the middle of the tunnel for thirty minutes. But nothing happened. I was fine. I didn't panic at all."

That was a few years ago. Recently, Carole reported she had just traveled through the Chesapeake Bay Bridge-Tunnel, excitedly saying it was twelve miles long and she "didn't feel a thing!" Carole's regulation systems, boosted by links to calming memories, worked well.

Our arousal-regulating system is called the *autonomic nervous system*. *Auto* is a Greek prefix meaning "self." *Nomic* means "management" or "control." Thus the name refers to a self-regulating system, the part of our nervous system that operates automatically outside our conscious control. The autonomic nervous system has two parts, one that revs us up and another that calms us down.

The sympathetic nervous system automatically revs us up when stress hormones are released. The part of the brain responsible for releasing these hormones is the amygdala. It is often said that the amygdala responds to threats, or to danger. That is misleading. It is more accurate to say the amygdala responds to change. The amygdala cannot tell what is and is not a threat, or what is or is not dangerous. By far, most of the changes the amygdala responds to are inconsequential.

The amygdala can be compared with the brake lights of a car ahead of you in traffic. Illumination of the brake lights mean change: the car is slowing. Is this a threat? It depends how close you are to the car and how rapidly it is slowing down. Like the brake lights, the amygdala alerts you to change. The amygdala cannot determine what you need to do about the change. That is the job of the thinking part of your brain.

The calming part of the autonomic nervous system is the parasympathetic nervous system. Its key component is the vagus nerve. *Vagus* is a Latin word that means "wandering." This nerve wanders through the chest and abdomen, connecting the heart and the organs of the digestive system to the brain. When the vagus nerve is stimulated, it overrides the effects of stress hormones and decreases the heart rate. The neuroscientist Stephen Porges refers to this process as *vagal braking.* As this happens, you may feel your guard letting down, a reflex caused when we receive signals from a person that they are no threat to us in any way.

Panic happens only when automatic regulation of arousal is not working. When you start to experience panic, you may try to control your reaction consciously. But that may not work, for two reasons. First, your capacity for conscious thought, located in the cortex, breaks down when stress hormones build up. Second, conscious thought may not activate the parasympathetic nervous system. The solution to panic is to train your unconscious procedural memory, located in the subcortex, to calm you automatically, by repeating the exercises in this book.

First, we train your unconscious procedural memory to keep your sympathetic nervous system from getting you revved up in situations that might trigger panic. Unconscious procedural memory can be taught to automatically release oxytocin, and thus to block the release of stress hormones when you are in a panic-provoking situation.

Second, we train your unconscious procedural memory to activate the parasympathetic nervous system any time you begin to panic. The parasympathetic nervous system will automatically apply vagal braking to override the effects of stress hormones.

Either of these trained responses can be used independently to control panic. When your unconscious procedural memory has learned to use both, panic doesn't have a chance.

CHAPTER 4

How Carole Used a Memory to Calm Herself Automatically

How would you like to have a switch that could simply turn off your panic attacks? We can set one up, using a system you were born with. Your parasympathetic nervous system can override stress hormones. It can stop a panic attack in its tracks. All you need is a way to turn it on using the right kind of memory.

What kind of memory can do this? Surprisingly, the answer is not recollection of a happy time or a day relaxing on the beach. At those times, we are relaxed — not because the parasympathetic nervous system is actively calming us, but because the amygdala finds no cause to release stress hormones. We need a memory that activates your parasympathetic nervous system, and calms you in spite of things going on that stress you.

What activates the parasympathetic nervous system? Think for a moment about what a mother does to calm a crying infant. She presents her face. Her soft, loving smile activates the infant's parasympathetic nervous system. She speaks to the baby. Though the baby does not understand her words, the baby's parasympathetic nervous system responds to the quality of her voice. In addition, touch — being held or caressed — activates the young child's parasympathetic nervous system. So there is your answer. The parasympathetic nervous system is activated by face, voice, and touch, provided that the signals being sent are calm, attuned, and caring.

We don't need to go back to infancy: we don't remember that far back. But we can use any memory we can recall of being with a close, trusted friend, ideally at a time when we felt our guard let down. Note that when you feel your guard let down, you don't cause it consciously: it happens unconsciously when the vagus nerve, fully stimulated, releases all the tension present in your body.

In most social situations, we receive signals that we are physically safe. But because people are often competitive and judgmental, the signals they unconsciously send, and which we unconsciously receive, can keep us from feeling emotionally safe. We remain careful about what we say; we do not reveal our private thoughts or genuine feelings. We may even employ a facade to hide behind and protect our real self from being judged by others. But with a good friend, who does not judge us, we may at times feel our guard let down. This happens, according to Porges, when the signals we unconsciously receive are optimal, and cause us to feel physically and emotionally safe.

This was the experience we wanted to evoke when Carole took her drive. To make sure her vagus nerve would be stimulated repeatedly, she linked landmarks along the way to memories of a time with a friend with whom she felt her guard let down. First, Carole remembered being with her friend, and then she imagined that her friend was holding up a photograph of one of the landmarks. By picturing her friend's face juxtaposed with the photograph, Carole established a visual link between the calming face and the landmark. Next, Carole imagined that she and her friend looked at the landmark photograph together and exchanged a few words about the photograph. This linked her friend's calming voice to the landmark. Finally, she imagined that as they looked at the photograph together, her friend gave her a reassuring touch, which was also linked to the landmark. Carole continued this process until each landmark had visual, auditory, and physical links to her friend's calming presence. As Carole took her trip, each landmark she passed, linked to the memories of her friend, activated vagal braking and kept her calm.

This technique can help you regulate arousal in situations that have previously caused anxiety or even panic. Like Carole, you can break the challenging situation down into a series of events or steps and link each of them to a memory of a time when you felt both physically and emotionally safe. This activates your vagus nerve and calms your mind and body.

CHAPTER 5

How Arousal Regulation Works

If you are skeptical about the power of Carole's memory of a friend's face, voice, and touch, you might be persuaded by some research on smiles. There are two kinds of smiles. First, there is an intentional "social smile." In a social smile, a person consciously activates muscles at the corners of their mouth. Second, there is a genuine smile that happens spontaneously. In a genuine smile, the muscle that surrounds the eye — the orbicularis oculi — contracts. This muscle cannot be operated intentionally. Since contraction of the orbicularis oculi is strongly associated with delight, returning a spontaneous smile causes you to feel delight. A spontaneous smile is called a *Duchenne smile*, after the nineteenth-century French scientist Duchenne de Boulogne, who discovered the physiological and emotional differences between a social and a genuine smile.

When someone smiles at you, you reflexively return the type of smile you received. When someone flashes you their best social smile, the smile you reflexively return — lacking operation of the orbicularis oculi — produces no delight. If you have just gotten Botox injections for smile lines around your eyes and feel less pleasure when greeted by friends, now you know why. Botox can keep those delight-linked muscles from contracting. By contrast, when a friend is delighted to see you, muscles surrounding their eyes operate spontaneously. You reflexively return their spontaneous smile with a spontaneous smile of your own.

If you can think back to the feeling of delight you experienced when seeing and reflexively returning a genuine, spontaneous smile, you may begin to trust that unconscious processes involving the face can change what you feel in other ways. This chapter examines the neurological mechanisms that govern our responses to our world and make these changes possible.

The sympathetic nervous system, the system that increases arousal, does not require development. It works naturally. Every newborn baby is fully capable of getting revved up and screaming bloody murder (a state known as *hyperarousal*). But newborns cannot calm themselves by activating their own parasympathetic nervous system: it can be activated only by others. Babies are genetically programmed to be calmed by others who present an attuned face, a calm voice, and a loving touch.

As the child's brain develops, it retains memories of the caregiver's face, voice, and touch. If a caregiver responds consistently when the child is upset, the child comes to expect that the caregiver will appear to calm her. Anticipating this response, she imagines the caregiver's face, voice, and touch. This imagination immediately activates the calming parasympathetic nervous system. The child is calm before the caregiver even reaches the child.

What happens next is important. If the child's caregiver follows through with a calming response, the child's expectations are reinforced, and a program begins to form in her unconscious procedural memory. The program has four steps. First, hyperarousal causes her to wish for her caregiver. Second, because her caregiver is dependable, she expects the caregiver to appear. Third, she imagines her caregiver's face, voice, and touch. Fourth, imagination activates her calming parasympathetic nervous system. In other words, hyperarousal causes expectation, which causes imagination, which activates calming.

If these four steps are established as a program in the child's unconscious procedural memory, hyperarousal will be automatically down-regulated to alertness throughout her life. She will not be subject to panic. Automatic down-regulation will allow her to think clearly under stress.

If, however, the caregiver does not respond as the child expects, there is no reinforcement, and automatic down-regulation is not established. Paradoxically, it is also possible that the program may not be established if the caregiver acts too quickly. The psychological theorist Heinz Kohut believed that "the most important aspect of the earliest mother-infant relationship is the principle of optimal frustration." Automatic down-regulation develops when a child meets with some difficulty, acts to deal with the difficulty, and is successful. When things work too smoothly, there is no reason for a child to act. For example, if a caregiver calms a child before the child is frustrated enough to need the caregiver, summon her, imagine her response, and thus trigger the parasympathetic nervous system, no program to automatically down-regulate arousal will develop. On the other hand, if the child meets with too much frustration, the child learns that action is futile, and automatic down-regulation does not develop.

In any case, a child who does not develop automatic down-regulation is likely to fear hyperarousal. As an adult, they may need to be in control of every situation so that no hyperarousal takes place. They may need to avoid situations unless escape — a basic way to down-regulate hyperarousal — is available as a backup strategy if they lose control of the situation.

To understand how emotional regulation evolved, Stephen Porges suggests we look back two hundred million years, long before mammals arrived on the scene and even longer before humans made their entrance. At that time, the most highly evolved creatures were reptiles. The reptile's amygdala monitored the environment for any kind of change, such as the presence of unfamiliar creatures. On encountering a new creature, the amygdala triggered the release of stress hormones that caused an urge to run away.

This was a useful response when the new creature was dangerous, because it protected the reptile from harm. But not every change or new creature was dangerous. Let's imagine that an apatosaurus showed up. Being a vegetarian, the apatosaurus posed no threat to another reptile. Yet the amygdala still fired off stress hormones, and with no thinking part of the brain to deter this urge, the reptile followed the urge and ran away.

This primitive system, which Porges calls the *mobilization system*, produced a lot of false alarms. These were costly to the creature. Running away burns calories. In searching for food to replace those calories, Porges points out, the creature had to expose itself to additional dangers. Also, escape itself could result in injury — for example, the creature might fall over a cliff or be attacked by a more dangerous predator. The mobilization system's protection was less than ideal.

As mammals evolved, they developed larger brains. Their capacity for thought provided more sophisticated protection. When a mammal's amygdala released stress hormones, the hormones still produced an urge to run. But the stress hormones also activated the thinking and decision-making part of the mammal's brain — the part we now refer to as *executive function*. The mammal's executive function inhibited the urge to run and assessed the situation to determine whether escape was necessary. If it found that the change the amygdala was reacting to was not a threat, it signaled the amygdala to end the release of stress hormones.

Fast forward to humans. When you see a stranger, your amygdala-based mobilization system produces the urge to escape, just as it did in prehistoric reptiles. Simultaneously, the stress hormones activate your executive function, the high-level thinking that makes decisions. To give you time to look the stranger over, executive function overrides the urge to run. Tension develops as one part of the brain — the amygdala — tells you to run, and another part — executive function — tells you to hold on.

Meanwhile, something else is going on. You are exchanging unconscious signals with the stranger. If these signals indicate that the stranger is not a physical threat, your brain stimulates the vagus nerve to some degree. This slows your heart rate and overrides the effects of the stress hormones, causing you to relax. These signs that you are physically safe end the sense of alarm and set the stage for cooperation with this new friend (assuming that your brain interpreted the exchange of signals correctly).

This system, which Porges calls the *social engagement system*, allows two people to feel comfortable together. Down-regulating signals from our social engagement system helps us work together, live together, and mate. To understand how the social engagement system can override stress hormones, think of being in a car with an automatic transmission, with one foot planted solidly on the brake pedal. If the other foot presses on the accelerator and sends more gas into the engine, the brake keeps the car in place.

Porges refers to this overriding by the vagus nerve as *vagal braking*. Just as the brake pedal can slow your car down — even when gas is being pumped into the engine — the vagal brake can calm you down even when the amygdala is pumping stress hormones into you.

When you receive signals that the person you are with is not a physical threat, the vagus nerve causes you to feel physically safe. But when you receive signals that you are emotionally as well as physically safe, profound calming takes place. You feel your guard let down. This response is unconscious, a result of maximum vagal braking. We can use this response to prevent panic.

When psychology was a new science, the central importance of relationship to human development was not understood. "Nobody then anticipated *how* dependent the infant's *brain* was on the mother's caregiving and social interaction," wrote the psychiatrist James Grotstein. Gradually, as psychology matured, researchers demonstrated the importance of bonds with others, particularly in early childhood. In the mid-twentieth century, the psychologist Carl Rogers founded a therapy movement aimed at adults that was based on "unconditional positive regard." In the 1960s, experiments by Harry Harlow showed that baby monkeys preferred soft dolls they could cuddle with over hard dolls made of wire that provided milk. Following that, research by John Bowlby showed that infants need relationship and are genetically programmed to seek it. The theorists Anthony Bateman and Peter Fonagy now tell us that every child is "constitutionally primed to find a version of their internal states mirrored by their caregivers."

It's easy to see your physical self: just look in a mirror. But how do we get a sense of who we are as a person? Our psychological self develops based on the way others respond to us when we express our thoughts, our ideas, our needs, and our feelings. Their response is like a mirror. It tells us who they think we are, and whether — to them — we are valuable or not. While the way others respond to us as adults has an effect on us, the way parents respond to a child early in life forms the child's sense of self and the child's emotional regulation. These develop in tandem, and both are relationship dependent.

Our identity and our emotional regulation develop based on relationships during our formative years. Good emotional regulation cannot develop if a child cannot count on physical and psychological safety. The need for physical safety is obvious, but parents may fail to understand how to provide psychological safety. If the child's need for safety is not met, the child may develop into an adult who controls hyperarousal by trying to control the situation he is in. If he is not in control and things don't go well, he cannot control his arousal. To regain control, he must fight to regain dominance or escape.

When a child is not afraid of the caregiver, the child feels safe in the caregiver's presence. But children also need to feel secure when their caregiver is not physically present. When the caregiver is absent, a secure child knows — because of the nature of their relationship — that the caregiver has him in mind, values him, and therefore will return to him. An insecure child, by contrast, is unsure about being valued or even wanted. The child feels abandoned when the caregiver is absent: out of sight, out of mind. Insecurity arrests the development needed to learn to regulate emotion and to prevent panic.

Fortunately, those of us who did not develop adequate emotional regulation during childhood can now pick up where its development left off. We can activate our calming parasympathetic nervous system by linking challenging situations that cause arousal, and the onset of arousal itself, to a person who — to use Carl Rogers's term — holds us in unconditional positive regard.

Think of being in an elevator surrounded by people you don't know. Your amygdala is sounding the alarm. Stress hormones create the urge to escape. Your primitive emotion-regulating system, the mobilization system, is saying, "Get out of here!" But your more sophisticated executive function pushes back as if to say, "You think you need to escape, but you don't. Just wait. We'll be out in a minute." As the elevator trip grinds on, the tension between the mobilization system and executive function, between the messages to flee and to stay, intensifies. We call this feeling *claustrophobia*.

Which system seems to be winning may depend on how crowded the elevator is. But — and this is important — it may also depend on seeing someone in the elevator who is not a stranger. Imagine that as you warily look around, you see a friend, the special friend who never judges you in any way. He or she is not just smiling, but beaming at you.

Maybe you unconsciously picked up the signal from that special face. Maybe that is why you felt comfortable enough to look around. Now, as you see each other, your friend is activating your social engagement system, the advanced system humans have that overrides the effects of the stress hormones when we receive signals of physical and emotional safety.

Your friend's presence changes everything. Strangers in the elevator become irrelevant. The urge to bolt disappears. The feeling of claustrophobia subsides.

In an elevator or anywhere else, the amygdala reacts to the presence of strangers and triggers the release of stress hormones. Just as they did two hundred million years ago, stress hormones produce an urge to escape. But until the elevator stops and its door opens, we can't relieve the stress. Our high-level thinking, executive function, tries to reason with us and tell us there is no cause for fear. In some people, executive function is so well developed that it completely inhibits the urge to escape; they have no awareness of discomfort. But not everyone has such robust executive function. Most people feel some discomfort. Some of us feel a lot.

Here is where the social engagement system can step in and make the elevator ride comfortable. If we receive the right signals from another person, the social engagement system activates the parasympathetic nervous system. It applies vagal braking, which overrides the stress hormones and makes us feel at ease.

But what if there is no one physically present whose face, voice, and touch have that effect? Research at the University of Arizona, published in 2019, shows that having a calming friend in mind is as protective against stress as having the friend physically present. The research involved 102 participants who were in a committed romantic relationship. Participants were split into three groups. Members of each group were exposed individually to a stressful situation. In the stressful situation, those in the first group were asked to think about their day. Those in the second group were asked to think about their romantic partner. Those in the third group had their partner present. Those assigned to the second and third groups had lower blood pressure during stress than those in the first group. There was no difference in the blood pressures of those in the second and third groups. One of the researchers, Kyle Bourassa, said, "It appears that thinking of your partner as a source of support can be just as powerful as actually having them present." The conclusions of this research study, regarded as groundbreaking, correspond with the results thousands of clients have achieved using the method in this book.

When Carole drove through the tunnel, she had no one physically with her to down-regulate her. Prior to her trip, however, she had made sure she had someone with her psychologically. She linked her trip through the tunnel, landmark by landmark, to the memory of a person whose face, voice, and touch activated her parasympathetic nervous system. Vagal braking calmed her. This method can be applied to any stress-producing situation.

CHAPTER 6

Control Panic and Claustrophobia with Vagal Braking

Becky emailed:

I have been terrified of elevators. As a nurse, I would climb ten or more flights of stairs at the hospital to avoid taking the elevator. This is part of a severe generalized anxiety disorder that resulted in years of daily panic attacks. I am fifty-two years old, and after seeing a variety of therapists over many years, this [the SOAR program] has helped me tremendously.

Carole's experience navigating the Holland Tunnel proves that we can intentionally evoke the effects of a friend's calming presence to manage panic. In some cases, calming signals from other people are built into our memories serendipitously. For example, even if you were scared when you first used an elevator, if you were with someone you felt physically and emotionally safe with, you likely associated that person's presence — and their calming signals — with the elevator. Thereafter, when in an elevator, the invisible psychological presence of that person quelled your fears. Your friend's psychological presence overrode the urge to escape and stopped the panic before it even started.

But if calming associations were not built into your brain serendipitously earlier in life, you can build them in now, as Carole did. It's really simple. We need to find a memory of a time when you were with a person whose presence activated your parasympathetic nervous system. Do you have a friend with whom you have, at times, felt your guard let down? If so, you were unconsciously receiving signals that you were physically and emotionally safe in their presence. Feeling your guard let down is proof of full activation of the parasympathetic nervous system. If you are not sure whether you have ever experienced this feeling, let me see if I can point you to it. When you are with a friend you feel comfortable with, you may think you are completely relaxed. Unexpectedly, a ripple goes through your body, and you relax even more. That's your guard letting down.

If you have not experienced this feeling, you can use something close to it: the memory of being with a person who, at least sometimes, did not judge you in any way. You may remember a child who was delighted to see you and ran to greet you. Other memories that may evoke the feeling are saying your wedding vows, getting engaged, cuddling a pet or seeing it running free, going fishing or playing golf with a friend, or celebrating a success with teammates.

To address the claustrophobia in an elevator, recall being with your friend. Remember their face, their eyes, their voice, and their touch. Imagine your friend is holding up a black-and-white snapshot of an elevator. Keep that in mind for a few seconds to establish a visual link between the elevator and the friend's face. Some signals that activate your calming system are communicated in a person's voice, so we also want to establish a vocal link. Imagine that you and your friend are looking at the snapshot together and having a conversation about it. It doesn't matter what is said: the important thing is that you link your friend's voice to the elevator scene in the photograph. Touch is calming, too: during this conversation, imagine that your friend gives you a reassuring touch.

Most panic-inducing situations have something in common: we feel unsafe, and escape is not immediately available. When escape is blocked, flight — our most instinctive way of dealing with panic — is compromised. After you have linked a calming memory of a friend to the experience of being in an elevator, consider other situations where escape is not immediately available such as a tunnel, a high place, a multilane highway, or a seat in a classroom, church, or theater that is not at the end of a row. All of these situations can be dealt with in the same way, by establishing calming links to them.

Everyone tries to avoid thinking about anxiety-producing situations. Set that strategy aside for a few minutes and make a detailed list of situations you find challenging. Choose one situation to work on. Think through all the parts of the experience. Link the face, voice, and touch of the calming friend to each challenging moment of the situation. Repeat this exercise daily for a week. Then choose another anxiety-producing situation, and work through that. Once you have linked all the challenging moments of each situation to the calming presence of your friend, you will no longer feel the urgent need to escape. If you have had your friend with you in a challenging situation and not felt calm, here is some good news: having your friend built inside, already linked directly to each challenging moment, provides greater calming than simply having the person with you physically but not linked to the challenges. Built inside, your friend stops the stress before you can become aware of it.

For the experience of getting in an elevator, I've listed some typical steps below. Your own list may be longer or shorter.

- Walking into the building
- Walking to the elevator
- Pressing the button for the elevator to come
- Waiting for the elevator
- Elevator door opening
- Seeing the elevator ready for you to get in
- Stepping into the elevator
- Selecting the tenth floor
- In the elevator; more people getting in
- In the elevator, waiting for the door to close
- Elevator door closing
- Elevator, with the door closed, not moving
- Elevator starting upward; heavy feeling
- Elevator passing the third floor
- Elevator passing the fifth floor
- Elevator passing the eighth floor
- Elevator slows its ascent; light-headed feeling
- Elevator stops; the door is still closed
- In the elevator; the door is opening
- In the elevator with someone blocking your exit
- In the elevator with no one in your way
- Stepping out of the elevator on the tenth floor
- Walking around the tenth floor

- Thinking about returning to the elevator
- Walking toward the elevator
- Pressing the button for the elevator to come
- Waiting for the elevator to arrive
- Elevator door opening
- Seeing the elevator ready for you to get in
- Stepping into the elevator
- Selecting the ground floor
- Others getting in the elevator
- Waiting in the elevator
- Elevator door closing
- Elevator door closed; not moving
- Elevator starts downward; light-headed feeling
- Elevator passing the eighth floor
- Elevator passing the fifth floor
- Elevator passing the third floor
- Elevator stopping; feeling physically heavy
- Elevator stops; the door is still closed
- In the elevator with the door opening
- In the elevator with someone blocking your exit
- In the elevator with no one in your way
- Leaving the elevator; one foot out, one foot still in
- Just outside the elevator
- Heading for the building exit
- Leaving the building
- Outside the building

CHAPTER 7

Control Panic and Claustrophobia with Oxytocin

Gretchen grew up in an area of Europe where there were no escalators. The combination of unfamiliarity and the inability to escape from a moving escalator led to trouble. Here's how she described her experience and her strategy for managing her fear.

I came to New York from Europe. I wasn't used to escalators and developed a fear of tall ones, mainly in the subways. I sometimes avoid these escalators and take the long stairs.

A week ago, I was in front of such an escalator. I decided I would go on it anyway. I waited for someone to come on so I could stand right behind them (this way I wouldn't see the stairs all the way up). Right after getting on the escalator, I felt some panic. I held the sides with both hands and was rather anxious. I decided to think of techniques to ease the stress. I tried counting down from one thousand, but that did not seem to work. So then I decided to use the oxytocin technique. I started thinking about nursing my kids. Immediately my breathing stabilized and I felt more relaxed, and the rest of the climb went fast. So it seems to work in this situation and provided fast relief. I am looking forward to trying this technique in other places as well.

We know that calming memories can override the effects of stress hormones. But even better, it's possible to *prevent* the release of stress hormones in the first place.

By releasing stress hormones, the amygdala alerts us to changes that might mean danger. Stress hormones can also prepare us to escape or to fight if the changes turn out to mean danger. Thus the release of stress hormones has value for individual survival. But from the perspective of evolution, individual survival is less important than reproduction, which enables our species to survive. This requires physical intimacy, which in turn requires that the "fight or flight" response be put on hold. The hormone oxytocin blocks the release of stress hormones that cause the "fight or flight" response.

Just as the memory of a calming friend can override stress hormones, the memory of an oxytocin-producing experience can prevent the release of stress hormones and feelings of panic and claustrophobia. Oxytocin is produced in the following situations:

1. **Sexual foreplay.** If the signals are right, oxytocin sets aside the fears of acting on our desire.
2. **Sexual afterglow.** Oxytocin causes feelings of attachment between sexual partners, making it more likely

that a child will have two parents to provide care and protection.

3. **The first sight of a newborn baby.** Oxytocin causes bonding and protective feelings toward the infant.

4. **Breastfeeding.** By inhibiting anxiety about other things that need to be done, oxytocin gives priority to a baby's need for nourishment.

5. **Gazing into your dog's eyes.** We say that lovers look at each other with "puppy dog eyes," as if there were no one else in the world. By looking at their owners with complete devotion, dogs tap into the chemistry that causes these feelings of attachment.

6. **Hugging.** Oxytocin is produced when a hug continues for twenty seconds or more.

When Carole and I were preparing for her trip through the Holland Tunnel, she identified landmarks she would see every few minutes on her trip and linked each landmark to her memory of an oxytocin-producing situation. This was similar to the way an intravenous pump can administer small, frequent doses of anti-anxiety or pain medication. Regular releases of oxytocin kept Carole calm throughout her trip.

Using *both* oxytocin production and vagal braking combats high anxiety and panic in two ways. Oxytocin inhibits the release of stress hormones. The vagal brake overrides their effects. In addition to linking each challenging situation to a friend whose calming presence stimulates your vagus nerve, try linking each challenge to a memory that triggers the release of oxytocin.

Part III

Regulation of Arousal

CHAPTER 8

Accepting Arousal as Normal

We've covered how to teach your unconscious procedural memory to automatically control panic that is triggered by something happening *around* you. You can also learn to control panic caused by something going on *inside* you. This is important because although you may be able to run away from an external threat, you can't run away from what goes on inside.

To avoid feeling trapped by what is going on inside, every child needs to learn that arousal is normal and that the feelings produced by arousal are normal. Only a caregiver can help the child learn this lesson. In addition, by responding to the child's arousal in an attuned, calm, and nonjudgmental way, the caregiver's response stimulates the child's vagus nerve, which calms the child through vagal braking.

If the caregiver does not respond calmly, the response may not produce vagal braking and may in fact lead to the opposite result. The caregiver's own hyperarousal becomes linked to what is going on inside the child and may cause completely normal feelings of arousal to trigger hyper-arousal, fear, and feelings of danger. This response may persist into adulthood.

The failure to experience states of arousal as completely normal can have a profound effect on a child's development. If caregivers respond negatively to the child's arousal, the child may be afraid of being punished or of what might happen if they become overwhelmed. The child may fear that arousal could produce feelings or behavior unacceptable to the caregiver, which could result in the caregiver's disapproval, loss of love, or abandonment.

How many of us have been shamed for "acting like a baby"? The child who learns to fear their own feelings is in a terrible bind. Pressured to not express emotion, the child seeks to keep emotion contained. But how does a child learn to control emotion when the caregiver does not demonstrate this capacity? Caregivers who pressure children about emotional control invariably lack emotional regulation themselves. As a result, they are unable to teach a child healthy ways to regulate emotion, either by example or by acting in a way that produces vagal braking in the child.

Dozens of studies have shown that the ability to regulate arousal develops from a child-caregiver relationship in which the caregiver is attuned and consistently responds to the child's arousal calmly and nonjudgmentally. This response produces vagal braking which, when linked in the child's mind to the situation or the emotion, establishes automatic emotional regulation in similar situations.

By contrast, a caregiver who is judgmental or critical of the child's emotions undermines the child's development of self-regulation. Responding to a child's emotional outbursts with punishment, such as spanking, can cause long-term damage. Researchers at the University of Texas at Austin conducted a meta-analysis of fifty years of research showing that spanking and child abuse produce the same results. One of the researchers, Elizabeth Gershoff, a professor of human development, said, "We as a society think of spanking and physical abuse as distinct behaviors. Yet our research shows that spanking is linked with the same negative child outcomes as abuse, just to a slightly lesser degree."

A caregiver who becomes hyperaroused in response to a child's arousal may force the child to shut down rather than self-regulate. A caregiver who withdraws when the child is aroused provides the child with no basis for feeling safe. Neither response establishes the links between arousal and vagal braking that are needed to develop healthy down-regulation of arousal.

Note, however, that regulation does not always mean down-regulation; it can also mean up-regulation. The developmental researcher Allan Schore, a leading authority on emotional regulation, asked therapists attending one of his workshops to imagine a mother playing with a little child, perhaps six months old. The child smiles; the mother reciprocates with a smile. That causes the child to giggle, which in turn causes the mother to giggle. The child responds to the mother's giggle with a laugh. Both become more and more aroused, perhaps almost unable to stop laughing. But because the mother and the child experience a high level of arousal together, the child learns that this is a normal, non-threatening experience. Thus arousal is unlikely to lead to panic in the future.

The wise caregiver enjoys sharing excitement with the child but does not try to keep the child in a prolonged state of high arousal. For example, tickling can be fun if it is brief, but too much tickling is intolerable. When the mother is at-tuned and responsive to the child's signals, stimulation is comfortable and delightful for both. The child learns that every level of arousal is part of the normal range and is tol-erable if experienced briefly.

Beatrice Beebe and Frank M. Lachmann have studied mother-child interactions in which mothers keep children highly aroused for too long. When the mother's stimulation becomes too much for the child, the child turns his head away. If the mother feels rejected, she may try harder to en-gage the child by increasing the stimulation. The child turns away as much as possible. If unable to escape the mother's overstimulation, the child becomes relationally trauma-tized and experiences ordinary arousal as an overwhelming threat. Because the child is helpless to defend against it, un-bearable intrusion may cause lifelong avoidance of close re-lationships and obstruct the normal operation of the social engagement system. The child, and later the adult, is afraid that feelings will develop that they cannot endure.

Teaching a child emotional regulation is like sharing a scary ride at Disney World. It's the caregiver's job to accom-pany the child on the real world's emotional roller-coaster rides. The psychiatrist and researcher Daniel Siegel has writ-ten, "Interactive experiences enable the child not only to ex-perience high levels of…arousal, but to entrain the circuits of the brain to be able to manage such states." When a care-giver and child share emotional experiences, they exchange conscious and unconscious signals that teach the child that all levels of arousal are normal, potentially pleasurable, and manageable.

Siegel goes on to say that it is important for the child to know that the caregiver feels what the child is feeling.

"Feeling felt…having the sense that someone else feels one's feelings and is able to respond contingently to one's communication may be vital to close relationships of all sorts throughout the lifespan."

Beebe and Lachmann write that an infant hungers for his experience to be matched by his caregiver: being on the same wavelength as the caregiver lays the groundwork for a child to feel known and secure. They studied a group of children who were severely insecure in their attachment to their mothers. The mothers did not try to match their child's emotional state or to let the child know that his feelings were understood and shared. Instead of acknowledging and matching the child's negative emotion, these mothers countered it. First, they dismissed the child's distress with a smile or with a look of surprise. Then they tried to move the child quickly to a positive emotional state. Though this might seem like a logical way to reduce a child's distress, Beebe and Lachmann believe that it causes a child to feel abandoned and alone. The caregiver is the infant's whole world. From the infant's perspective, if the caregiver does not share the child's experience, no one ever will.

We humans are creatures of relationship. Isolation is distressing. Self-awareness creates a hunger to share what we are aware of with others. When our fundamental need for relationship is stonewalled by those around us, we are at risk of depression.

Sharing our experience involves learning to identify and name emotions. Activities and objects are easily named because they can be pointed to. Naming emotions is more difficult. If the caregiver tells the child the name of the shared emotion, the child learns that the experience is known. If the caregiver shares the experience and remains emotionally regulated, the child also learns that the emotion is not dangerous. This shifts an experience from being unknown and threatening to being known and safe. In addition, as we have seen, the caregiver's attuned response stimulates the child's vagus nerve and calms the child neurologically. Thus, neurological calming becomes linked to the named and known experience.

When an emotion is not shared, it cannot be named: it remains unknown and potentially dangerous. Since the amygdala releases stress hormones when presented with anything unfamiliar, unshared and unnamed experiences are ongoing stressors that undermine the child's ability to develop self-regulation and a sense of personal security.

Since our most basic way of regulating ourselves is to approach what interests us and to distance ourselves from what threatens us, caregivers unskilled in other ways of emotional regulation tend to distance themselves from a child who causes them distress. Distancing leaves the child emotionally and perhaps physically abandoned. Caregivers who cannot distance themselves from a child who arouses them may retaliate verbally or physically to an emotion expressed by the child. If this happens, the child learns to associate emotional expression with abandonment or aggression by the caregiver. This in turn causes the child to equate arousal with fear, and fear with danger. According to Allan Schore, "This inaccessible caregiver reacts to her infant's expressions of emotions and stress inappropriately and/or rejectingly, and therefore shows minimal or unpredictable participation in the various types of arousal-regulating processes. Instead of modulating, she induces extreme levels of stressful stimulation and arousal."

A child whose caregiver accompanies her on life's early

emotional roller-coaster rides becomes curious rather than fearful when stress hormones are released. In contrast, a child who does not experience a calming presence often experiences arousal and fear as one and the same. A child left to ride the roller coaster alone has no way to learn self-regulation or calming. Even as an adult, he or she is anxious and insecure. Feelings of arousal trigger feelings of danger. Is it the situation that can't be controlled or escaped from, or is it the emotion? A person who has not learned emotional regulation does not have a way to differentiate the two.

CHAPTER 9

How Feelings of Security and Insecurity Develop

According to trauma therapist and researcher Bessel van der Kolk, secure kids "learn to trust both what they feel and how they understand the world." On the other hand, insecure children find the world disorganized and distressing. "If the distress is overwhelming, or when the caregivers themselves are the sources of the distress, children are unable to modulate their arousal...." How does a sense of security or insecurity develop? How does it affect a person's adult life? Let's consider two fictional adults I'm going to call Suzie and Ingrid. I chose those names so you can easily remember that Suzie, whose name starts with *S*, generally feels safe and secure; and Ingrid, whose name starts with *I*, feels insecure, often for no apparent reason.

When Suzie's amygdala triggers the release of stress hormones to call her attention to something unfamiliar, she experiences a surge of arousal. Because her caregivers have routinely responded to her when this happened in the past, the surge of arousal doesn't alarm her. Rather, it causes her to feel curious about what is going on. Curiosity causes her to look around. If she finds nothing amiss, she pauses for a moment and then drops the matter.

When a surge of stress hormones arouse Ingrid, she, unlike Suzie, experiences alarm. Because of past experience, she associates alarm with danger. She too tries to figure out what is going on, but her belief that there is danger makes it hard for her to assess the situation in a balanced way. If she can't identify the danger that she believes must exist, she begins to imagine what it might be. And as long as she continues to feel alarmed, she can't drop the matter.

We sometimes say that seeing is believing. In Ingrid's case, feeling is believing. Her sense of alarm makes her believe that there *must* be danger, even if she can't see what it is. She knows that her eyes can play tricks on her and make it appear something is true that isn't, but she regards her feelings as infallible. She doesn't understand that arousal is merely the way the amygdala gets her attention, sending her a signal that she needs to determine whether or not a danger exists. Instead of recognizing that stress hormones are signaling her to make a determination, she believes the determination has already been made. She believes feeling aroused or alarmed proves there is danger.

In other words, the amygdala releases stress hormones to grab a person's attention and direct their high-level thinking toward determining whether an unfamiliar situation poses a real threat. But Ingrid doesn't use her high-level thinking. When stress hormones hit, she feels alarmed. Lacking the mental programming to shift alarm to alertness, she stays alarmed. Because she feels alarmed, she feels afraid. Because she feels afraid, she believes there is danger. Her assessment of the situation is based not on high-level thinking but on emotion.

Though Ingrid has a huge frontal cortex capable of logical thought, her assessment of the situation is made by a part of the brain the size of a nut. What has led her to turn over control of her life to a part of her brain that can't think?

Suzie learned early in life to distinguish arousal, alarm, fear, and danger. Ingrid experiences all of these feelings as one and the same, fused by early trauma. Her early life may have been similar to that of a client who told me that when his father was sober, they got along fine. But when Dad started drinking, the client's arousal level increased sharply because he knew that sooner or later he was going to be hit. For him, feelings of arousal continued to mean fear and danger into adulthood.

Arousal, alarm, fear, and danger can be conflated even when a person has not experienced physical trauma. Julian Ford, professor of psychiatry at the University of Connecticut School of Medicine, explains that the most complex form of trauma is not physical but psychological. Psychological trauma involves "interactions with people who teach the child or adolescent to focus on danger and survival rather than on trust and learning." If these interactions occur early in childhood, while the brain is particularly malleable, "lasting changes in the personality and the self occur." Since arousal equals fear, and fear equals danger, stress hormones that trigger arousal cause alarm. When arousal occurs, instead of feeling curious and going into a learning mode, the person fears danger and goes into a survival mode. As an adult, the person is subject to "entrenched expectations of danger that lead to preoccupation with detecting and defending against threats." In short, inadequate automatic regulation of arousal, coupled with the belief that arousal means danger, can lead to panic.

In a person whose childhood arousal was responded to calmly by early caregivers, alarm is automatically down-regulated to alertness, interest, or curiosity. In a person with a history of relationships in which arousal led to and became associated with pain or injury, arousal must be regulated by being able to control what happens in the situation — or by being able to escape from the situation — to prevent possible pain or injury. Unable to depend on others for safety, the person believes that safety depends on their being in control or able to escape. The lack of control or a means of escape may lead to anxiety and panic.

When a house is built, plumbing and wiring are installed early in the process. Once installed, the pipes and wires are likely to remain unchanged for the life of the house. The same is true of the brain's wiring. Early relationships literally wire up a child's emotional-control circuitry. Here is how "neurons that fire together wire together." This phrase encapsulates the neurological theory presented by Donald Hebb in his 1949 book *The Organization of Behavior*. When adjacent neurons in the brain fire at the same time, they connect to each other and form a new circuit. Think of welding. If a red-hot piece of metal touches another piece of metal, the two pieces become attached. If an electrical current is then applied to one piece, it flows through the other as well.

Let's apply Hebb's axiom to relationship. When a mother smiles at a child, her smile causes millions of neurons to fire. Some neurons, those in close proximity when the firing takes place, connect. This causes a modification of the circuitry. Once firing together has led to wiring together, the signal that originally traveled along one neural pathway now travels along a second pathway as well. How does this get translated into emotional regulation? Let's try an oversimplified example. Let's imagine that Suzie and Ingrid are children heading to kindergarten for the first time. Both are going alone, without their mothers to calm them. Let's pretend they are both precocious and savvy about neuropsychology. Suzie might say something like this:

I'll be okay, Mom, because when I was younger, every time I felt upset, you tuned into me. You could tell what I was feeling. You showed me light at the end of the tunnel by telling me that, though I was upset, I would feel better in just a minute. Because you did this repeatedly, the neurons that fired when you calmed me wired together. Now, when I start to get upset, your face, voice, and touch automatically calm me.

At kindergarten, though you will not be with me physically, you will be with me psychologically. While I am away, you will have me in your mind, and I will have you in my mind. Even though we are in two different places, we will still be connected.

Suzie's memories of the many times her mother calmed her are stored like a video in her mind. Being upset automatically triggers the Play button, and the video plays in Suzie's unconscious procedural memory. As it does, Suzie unconsciously sees her mom's face. Her mom's soft eyes calm her. Suzie hears her mom's voice: "I know how you feel. It's okay. Everything's going to be fine." Suzie unconsciously feels her mother's reassuring touch. These memories activate Suzie's parasympathetic nervous system. Calming takes over, and soon everything is okay.

What about Ingrid? Her mother did not consistently respond to her meltdowns in a way that was calming. Sometimes she responded as Suzie's mother did, but at other times she did not respond at all. And sometimes she invalidated Ingrid's feelings, saying, "There's nothing to be upset about." or "Stop that crying or I'll give you something to cry about!"

When alarmed, Suzie seeks out her mother, a reliable haven of safety. But when Ingrid is alarmed, if she turns to her mother, she may be jumping from the frying pan into the fire. Research shows that children in Ingrid's predicament, having nowhere to turn, become more alarmed, and once alarmed, remain alarmed longer than other children. "Thus, not only is the onset of sympathetically driven fear-alarm states more rapid, but their offset is prolonged, and they endure for longer periods of time," according to Allan Schore.

When Ingrid is about to go off to kindergarten, she says:

> Look, Mom, if I have a meltdown at kindergarten, I don't know what I'll do. I have all these different recordings of you in my mind. When I hit the Play button, it's like Russian roulette. If the video of you loving me and calming me comes up, I'll be okay. But if a video of you invalidating me starts playing, I won't trust myself. And what if I start seeing a video of your threatening me or hitting me? I'm too anxious to bring you to mind. Since I can't depend on what is built inside to calm me psychologically, I need you to be there with me physically to do it.

Everyone is subject to the release of stress hormones and the resulting feelings of high arousal or alarm. Some of us have neural programming that activates automatically and calms us. We go from alarm to interest or curiosity about what the amygdala is reacting to. Those of us who don't have that software stay alarmed until the stress hormones burn off. We try to control our arousal by being in control of what is going on so that we can be sure there is nothing to get upset about. We tend to avoid situations where we can't control what happens. If we can't avoid such a situation, we make sure that if things go wrong, we can get out.

Fortunately, if our circuits for automatically attenuating alarm and regulating arousal — including panic — were not established in early childhood, we can establish them now. We can pick up where development left off.

Let's consider Ingrid again as an adult. On the surface, she looks cool, calm, and collected. Everyone thinks she has it all together. In part that may be because she has some good friends who are rarely competitive with each other. When she is with them, the signals she unconsciously picks up from them keep her parasympathetic nervous system active. She can let down her guard and feel completely comfortable.

When Ingrid starts a new job, however, there is competition among the employees. Her performance is subject to judgment and criticism. No one provides her with unconscious signals that all is well. Anxiety causes her to judge and criticize herself. But because Ingrid needs to control things to feel safe, she has become quite accomplished at it. Though she pays an emotional price for it, this ability advances her career, and she becomes a manager.

Initially, she handles her new responsibilities well. But, as she advances and faces greater challenges, she can't control every detail. Stress builds up. She has occasional panic attacks and consults a therapist. The therapist asks her to

replace critical thoughts about herself with positive affir-
mations. The therapist also tells her that since panic attacks
cause no harm, she should not fear them.

Ingrid expected that therapy would make her feel better,
but being told by a person she believes is an authority that
she should not be troubled by panic attacks is one of the
most invalidating things that has ever happened to her. How
could she *not* mind having a panic attack? Does it mean
there is something wrong with her?

Though research has repeatedly shown that breathing
exercises do not relieve panic, the therapist recommended
them, probably because he was unwilling to admit to Ingrid
that he had no effective way to help her stop having panic
attacks. Though Ingrid didn't know it, the therapist had
set her up for failure. Her panic continued. When Ingrid's
health insurance carrier refused to pay for additional therapy sessions, she figured it was just as well. If anything, she
felt worse about herself after seeing the therapist.

To run well, a computer needs both good hardware and
good software. To attenuate alarm and regulate arousal, you
need good hardware; your brain needs to be physically in-
tact. Usually, nature takes care of that. But regulation also
requires good software, and nature provides only half of it.
Every baby is born knowing how to get revved up, but nature
does not provide built-in software for calming down. That
has to be installed through emotionally secure relationships
with caregivers. Ingrid's early relationships did not install
the software she needed.

Now let's assume that Ingrid did what you are doing:
she read this book. She was surprised to discover that many
people feel the way she does. She didn't think anything was
missing during her childhood. Though she didn't remember

as many childhood events as others seemed to, she believed things were fine. Nevertheless, since the exercises in this book looked interesting, she decided to try them.

Because of her friends, it was easy for her to remember times when she felt her guard let down. She recalled a friend's face and pretended the friend was holding a photograph of a work situation that caused distress. She then pretended that she and the friend looked at the photograph together and talked about it. The calming quality of her friend's voice permeated the scene in the photo. She could remember her friend's reassuring touch. Ingrid pretended she felt that touch as she and her friend talked about what was going on in the photograph.

On the following day, she pictured her friend holding a cartoon. The cartoon character was having a panic attack, feeling his heart pounding. In her imagination, Ingrid and her friend talked about that feeling. Remembering her friend's touch felt calming. Ingrid continued the exercise and linked each element of panic to her friend's face, voice, and touch.

To make the calming process more automatic, she practiced bringing her friend's face to mind whenever she noticed stress. As she practiced doing this, she was able to detect stress at lower and lower levels, which allowed her to nip it in the bud.

When she read the chapter on preventing panic attacks with the release of oxytocin, though, she ran into a problem. Where could she find a memory that produced oxytocin? She didn't have any experience of breastfeeding. She had held her cousin's newborn, but she hadn't experienced any remarkable sensation or emotion. Her romantic life had had its ups and downs. Currently, it was down. Although she had had strong feelings for someone, the relationship didn't work out, and the idea of recalling a moment of sexual fore-play didn't appeal to her. She had never had a pet whose eyes she could gaze into.

Ingrid decided to skip that exercise. Then, as she read on, she learned that even if a relationship ended badly, something of great value could be drawn from a memory of a time when things were good and fear of physical intimacy melted away. Ingrid was able to recall a good moment in one of her past relationships. By isolating that point in time — disregarding the before and after — she gained access to the kind of memory she needed. She linked that memory to the challenging situation at work and to the feelings that led to panic.

CHAPTER 10

Arousal Regulation Systems

Regulation of arousal involves several systems in our brains and bodies. To understand panic, we need to know a little about how they work. According to the neuroscientist Stephen Porges, regulation of arousal is first attempted by the most advanced system. If that system fails, regulation shifts to the next most sophisticated system, and so forth.

The Immobilization System

The most primitive system — the immobilization system — developed millions of years ago. It is responsible for "freeze" behaviors. Primitive creatures responded to threats by becoming immobile and appearing to be dead. Some creatures still respond in this way: the Annam stick insect, if touched, freezes and looks like a stick. Some beetles, if startled, become rigid. Some fall over, either pulling their legs in or sticking them up as if dead. Opossums not only "play dead" but also secrete a liquid that causes them to smell like a dead animal. Hog-nosed snakes also look and smell dead when threatened. When the immobilization system is activated in mammals, the heart rate and breathing rate slow so dramatically as to become imperceptible.

Porges points out that, though primitive, the immobilization system can serve creatures with small brains well. But in humans, the immobilization system is problematic. The human brain, being large, requires a high volume of blood flow. As immobilization reduces that blood flow, cognitive ability fades. Unable to think, a person may freeze, like a deer in the headlights. Then, as shutdown progresses, a person may faint or lose consciousness. In humans, Porges regards this primitive mechanism as our defense of last resort. Humans do not consciously choose to activate this system. It activates reflexively — even against our will — in life-threatening situations where it is futile to fight or to try to escape. Because cognitive ability can vanish, a woman may become unexpectedly unable to act when sexually assaulted, unless she has been trained to act automatically to protect herself. Since activation of the mobilization system is not widely understood, women who did not try to fight back or flee when sexually assaulted have sometimes been regarded as complicit. But, when the immobilization system shuts down the thinking part of the brain, it becomes impossible to fight — or at least to fight effectively — unless defensive action has been programmed into unconscious procedural memory by training. Similarly, it may not be possible for a person under extreme stress to flee unless an escape route is directly in view. If the thinking part of the brain has been incapacitated, the person may be unable to recognize the escape route and use it.

The Mobilization System

Unlike the first defensive system, which down-regulates arousal when threatened, the second defensive system up-regulates arousal when threatened. It is known as the mobilization system. If the amygdala senses change in the environment, it triggers a release of stress hormones that cause an urge to run away or to fight. Mobilization offers advantages over the immobilization system, which succeeds only if a predator fails to notice the immobile creature or loses interest because the creature appears dead.

But mobilization has a drawback. The amygdala cannot assess whether a change in the environment represents a true threat, so it can trigger the response to run away or fight even when no actual danger exists. Unnecessary flight wastes calories that must be replaced. Unnecessary fighting may result in injury or death. In humans, since the immobilization system is problematic, and is not used voluntarily, we think of the mobilization system as our most basic system of regulation. It requires no development other than the ability to use our own two feet to approach what interests us and to move away from what concerns us.

Executive Function

A third system developed when mammals came onto the scene. Increased mental ability allowed mammals to detect false alarms and avoid unnecessary mobilization. In addition to creating an urge to flee, the release of stress hormones, triggered by the amygdala, activates a decision-making capacity called executive function. When activated, executive function inhibits the urge to run, identifies what the amygdala is reacting to, determines whether the threat is real, and seeks a strategy that, by avoiding unnecessary running or fighting, conserves energy and reduces the risk of injury or death.

When executive function identifies a threat, if it can commit to a plan to deal with the threat, it signals the amygdala to stop the release of stress hormones, and goes forward with its plan. If executive function cannot identify a threat, it signals the amygdala to stop releasing stress hormones and drops the matter.

The catch with executive function is that, as we have seen, the amygdala reacts the same way to imaginary threats as it does to real threats. The job of differentiating between the two is carried out by *reflective function*, a subsystem of executive function that looks inward to sense what kind of mental processing is going on. If reflective function informs executive function that the amygdala is reacting to an imaginary threat, executive function dismisses the threat. Otherwise, executive function regards the threat as something it must reckon with.

When we are calm, reflective function has no trouble determining what is real and what is imaginary. But stress hormones can cause reflective function to collapse, especially if it is not well developed. In that case, an imaginary threat may be experienced as a real threat. In an elevator, for example, thinking "What if the elevator gets stuck?" triggers the release of stress hormones. If those hormones incapacitate our reflective function, we experience the imagined situation of being stuck as if it were really happening. Similarly, imagination of a heart attack may be experienced as a real heart attack. In a high place, the thought of falling feels like falling. An imagined experience, if mistaken as real, can result in terror and panic.

The Social Engagement System

Another brake on our arousal system is the social engagement system. Calming signals from another person can override the effects of stress hormones and cause us to feel safe. Development of the social engagement system requires an extended period of secure relationship with caregivers during early childhood.

A baby's arousal system, the sympathetic nervous system, is activated when stress hormones are released by the amygdala. The infant also has a calming system, the parasympathetic nervous system. But, as we have seen, unlike the arousal system, which is activated from within, the baby's calming system must be activated — at least for some time — from outside, through social engagement with caregivers.

The Internal Replica System

Our most advanced system for regulating arousal is based on what Allan Schore calls "internalized representations of relationships." These representations contain neural programming that regulates arousal.

This is a complex subject. But since internal representation can prevent panic, I'm going to offer a simplified explanation of what I call the "internal replica system."

Healthy regulation of arousal is dependent on a well-developed system that can override the effects of stress hormones both when we are alone and when we are with people who are not attuned or are not offering helpful signals. The internal replica system consists of working models of relationships with people who are important to us. Each replica represents our interactions with one person. Depending on the qualities of the relationship, the internal replica stabilizes (or destabilizes) us as it is dynamically overlaid onto the present situation.

The most important replica is a model of the relationship with the person's primary caregiver. The replica of the relationship includes encoded memories of the process by which your caregiver calmed you when you were a young child. As we have learned, when a child is aroused by the release of stress hormones, he or she can be calmed by a caregiver who responds in a composed, attuned, and nonjudgmental manner. The caregiver's presence activates the child's vagal brake within the calming parasympathetic nervous system. If arousal is consistently met with this response, a replica of the caregiver's calming response is built into the child's neural programming. It allows the caregiver to be psychologically present — that is, actively calming the child through the code embedded in the replica — even when the caregiver is not physically present. This system continues to stabilize or destabilize the person emotionally as an adult, even when the caregiver is no longer alive.

An internal replica will include the caregiver's way of responding when the child was aroused or alarmed. It may link a caregiver's calming presence to memories of specific challenges, such as climbing on playground equipment, skating, riding a bike, and interacting with other children.

Here's an example. When I was a child, my grandmother ran a florist business in the house where I lived with my parents. A resident employee, Ennis Merritt, eleven years my senior, was a sort of big brother. As the only child in a religious family, I was subject to constant judgment, and I was often anxious about the next words coming my way from my parents and grandparents. But Ennis had no interest in judging my behavior. When it rained, he was freed from his work tending flowers in the garden. He and I would sit side by side on the wide, cushioned glider on the covered front porch and watch the rain fall. If it was cool, we covered up with one of my grandmother's quilts. We sometimes sat there for hours, swinging gently. A North Carolina cloudburst could fill the street inches deep in water. As the rain fell, the water splashed upward from the puddles. Ennis called the splashes "jumping jacks." Without my knowing it, Ennis's attuned and nonjudgmental presence became strongly associated with rain for me.

Almost twenty years later I was in the Air Force, stationed in Europe, and I owned a race car. In Europe, races are not canceled because of rain. Most drivers are terrified of racing in the rain, but I found it more comfortable than racing in good weather. When, many years later, I learned of the internal replica system, I realized that Ennis's presence, tightly linked in my mind to rain, had made it possible for my executive function to operate a race car calmly at one hundred miles per hour in the rain. This example shows how powerful the internalized presence of another person can be.

It only takes one person. Daniel Siegel, MD, has said, "What studies of resilience show is that even when children have insecure attachment in the home, if they've had at least one secure attachment with a day care provider, preschool teacher, or another adult in their life, then that makes a huge difference for them having the seed of resilience. They may still have difficulty, but because they've had that one secure relationship, that relationship where they felt that another individual…knows them, feels what goes on inside them, those kids had the potential to do very well in the future."

For our internal replica system to calm us unconsciously, it requires only one person. This is because it takes only one person to activate our calming parasympathetic nervous system. A fortunate child, by being with such a person when engaged in activities, serendipitously establishes links between the calming person's presence and various activities. A person with a less fortunate childhood can establish calming links now. Even if you have not had a history of benevolent relationships during your formative years, if you can recall a moment with just one person who regarded you as a person and signaled that you were physically and emotionally safe in their presence, you can build an internal replica in which that moment of benevolent relationship is linked to the situations that emotionally challenge you.

Once again, even if you don't have this sort of history in general, it's not too late to find a moment that can be linked to your challenges. You can build a powerfully calming internal replica system now.

CHAPTER 11

The Arousal Regulation
Hierarchy

This chapter presents an overview of the systems that can
down-regulate hyperarousal and prevent panic. According
to Stephen Porges, down-regulation is attempted first by the
most advanced system. If something goes wrong and that
system fails, the task falls to the next most advanced system, and so forth down to the mobilization system, which
attempts to down-regulate by escape. If escape is blocked,
hyperarousal remains unregulated, and panic occurs.

The Internal Replica System

Since each internal replica is a working model of an actual
relationship, a replica can down-regulate hyperarousal just
as a calming person's physical presence can. When a replica
activates the parasympathetic nervous system, vagal braking causes down-regulation. This process takes place unconsciously.

What Can Go Wrong

- Adequate replicas are lacking or are not associated with the current challenge.
- A replicated person has recently become estranged from us or died. Until grieving softens the loss, replica activation may cause pain rather than down-regulation.
- Replicas of an abusive relationship destabilize rather than down-regulate.

If replicas fail to override the effects of stress hormones, a person may attempt down-regulation via the social engagement system by interacting with a real person.

The Social Engagement System

The social engagement system senses signals received unconsciously from others. When signals of safety activate the parasympathetic nervous system, vagal braking overrides the up-regulating effect of stress hormones. When the calming is profound, there may be a noticeable feeling of our guard letting down.

What Can Go Wrong

- No one is available to interact with.
- Fear of emotional involvement may obstruct interaction.
- Signals from the other person do not indicate safety.
- Signals that indicate safety are misinterpreted because of inexperience, past trauma, or neurological issues.

If the social engagement system fails to override the effects of stress hormones, regulation shifts to the next most sophisticated system, executive function.

Executive Function

Executive function temporarily inhibits the urge to take action, seeks to identify what caused arousal, and determines what action, if any, is needed. Commitment to a plan of action or to taking no action down-regulates arousal by signaling the amygdala to end the release of stress hormones.

What Can Go Wrong

- Executive function is unable to commit to a plan of action or to taking no action.

If executive function fails to end the release of stress hormones, regulation shifts to the mobilization system.

The Mobilization System

Continued release of stress hormones produces the urge to mobilize. This is sometimes called the "fight or flight response." If mobilization is successful, stress hormone release ends.

What Can Go Wrong

- The person is unable to combat the threat or to escape.

When the mobilization system is blocked and cannot relieve hyperarousal, panic may occur. If so, heart rate and breathing rate remain high. However, being trapped, or believing one is trapped, may involuntarily activate the immobilization system.

The Immobilization System

Activation of the immobilization system reduces breathing, slows the heart, and renders the person immobile. The supply of blood and oxygen to the brain is reduced. Impaired brain function may cause derealization, dissociation, and loss of sense of identity, location, and time. The person may believe they are dying. The mind, unable to keep up with what is happening, records only fragments of the event. This may produce enduring traumatic effects because a fragmented memory, unlike an ordinary memory, does not fade. As a result, the person may be subject to "flashbacks" in which a fragmented memory that lacks time information intrudes into awareness and is experienced as happening in the present. Flashbacks are one manifestation of post-traumatic stress disorder (PTSD).

Implications of Hierarchical Regulation

When hyperarousal takes place, the internal replica system attempts down-regulation. If it fails, the social engagement system takes over. If it also fails, executive function makes its attempt. Panic occurs only if all these systems fail to achieve down-regulation, because it occurs only at the lowest two levels, the mobilization and immobilization systems.

If even one of the advanced systems succeeds in down-regulating hyperarousal, the descent to the lower levels is avoided. Development of these systems is relationship dependent. The social engagement system is obviously based on experience with relationships. The replicas in the internal replica system are derived from actual relationships. Though executive function involves cognition, it depends on its subsystem, reflective function, to distinguish whether it is dealing with imagination or reality. Reflective function is also relationship dependent.

In the next chapter, we explore the "sweet spot" where executive function works best. Regulation of arousal is required to keep executive function in that sweet spot. To achieve better regulation, we have to improve the functioning of the advanced systems. Improvement depends, in one way or another, on relationship.

CHAPTER 12

Your Sweet Spot
for Stress Hormones

The brain needs a certain level of stress hormones to function at its peak. When we first wake up, our thinking is foggy. We drag out of bed and get going. Soon our body clock, perhaps with the help of a cup of coffee, will have us thinking more clearly.

But if something shocking happens, stress hormone levels may rise too high for peak cognitive function. Though we are wide awake, our high-level thinking is no better than when we first woke up. In addition, if stress hormones have disabled reflective function, we are no longer intuitively aware of what kind of mental processing is going on, which means imagination can be mistaken for reality. We may believe that our worst fears are coming to pass. And if we see no way to escape, we experience panic.

Anxiety is not panic. What's the difference? When we are aware that what we imagine may come to pass, that's anxiety. But if we experience a flood of stress hormones powerful enough to cause reflective function failure, then what we imagine becomes our reality. We believe that the thing we fear is really happening. If we also believe we can't escape, we panic.

For example, if we hyperventilate, imagining that we might suffocate can make us anxious. If imagination takes over, we believe we *are* suffocating. If we believe we cannot escape this experience, the mobilization system cannot regulate us, and the immobilization system takes over. That's panic.

All of us have out-of-control thoughts at times. If we worry that we might be going crazy, that is anxiety. But if out-of-control thoughts release enough stress hormones, reflective function collapses, imagination takes over, and we believe we *are* going crazy. If we can't find our way out of this belief, we feel trapped in insanity. The immobilization system takes over, and we panic.

Imagined danger can cause panic more easily than real danger. Once, counseling a client who was a lawyer, I wanted to help him recognize the difference between imaginary danger and real danger. I asked if he had ever been in a truly life-threatening situation. I was expecting him to come up with some imaginary situation that he had overreacted to, but he surprised me. He said a person had once come into his office and put a gun to his head. I had to agree with him that that was a genuinely life-threatening situation. I shifted gears, and asked him, "On a scale from 0 to 10 — with 0 being totally relaxed and 10 being the most anxiety you've ever felt — where were you while the gun was being held to your head?"

He said, "I was at a 2. But, the next day, I came to work and I went straight to a 10. I was a basket case. I couldn't do any work at all. So I went home. I came back to work the following day, and the same thing happened."

Why would a person experience only level 2 anxiety with an actual gun to their head, but level 10 when merely thinking about it? When the lawyer was being held at gunpoint, the situation was simple. He was forced to focus on one thing — the gun to his head — and nothing else. His amygdala reacted to the gun as a single unfamiliar situation and released only a single shot of stress hormones.

The next day was different. The attorney was free to imagine one gruesome scenario after another. For example, he could think, "What if that guy had pulled the trigger? I would be on the floor right there bleeding to death." His vivid imagination of the scene released a second shot of stress hormones which, added to the first, took him to 4 out of 10 on the anxiety scale. Then he imagined someone finding him and calling 911. He pictured himself in an ambulance being rushed to the hospital. That produced a third shot of stress hormones, which took him to level 6. He saw himself on a table in an operating room as his wife got a call telling her that he had been shot and it was not known whether he would survive. Imagining her anguish gave him another jolt of stress hormones. Imagining his daughter hearing the news and bursting into tears took him to a 10.

In real life, we experience only one outcome out of many possibilities. In our imagination, we can experience multiple outcomes, each of which can trigger the release of stress hormones. Imagination, then, can produce more stress than reality. Knowing that, some of us keep our imagination on a short leash, rarely allowing our mental scenarios to stray far from what is likely to happen. Others are less restrained. A psychiatrist I know, rather limited in how far he let his imagination go, was married to a woman whose imagination knew no bounds. Sometimes he would say to her, "Don't you realize how irrational that is?" It didn't alter her thinking. Early one morning, a neighbor knocked on their door. She had locked herself out of her house while stepping out to get the newspaper. The psychiatrist said, "No problem. I'll call a locksmith." But his wife interjected, "Why don't you try our key?"

The psychiatrist smirked. This was the chance he had waited for. His wife would at last recognize how irrational her ideas often were. So, saying nothing, he handed his wife a key. She went across the street with the neighbor, put the key in the lock, turned it, and the door opened! Her plan had worked. The psychiatrist said it taught him that he wasn't as much an authority on what is and isn't rational as he had thought.

If the prospect of an unlikely disaster comes to mind, most of us dismiss the thought as irrelevant. But a person whose imagination is freewheeling — like the psychiatrist's wife — can't easily stop worrying about things that are highly improbable.

For most urban professionals, obsessing about someone holding a gun to your head would be irrational because it is so highly unlikely. Nevertheless, that was the lawyer's experience. Is it irrational for him to now obsess about being shot? Yes, and no. On the one hand, he has firsthand evidence that it's possible. On the other hand, the fact that it happened yesterday does not increase the likelihood of its happening again today. Psychologically, however, it proves — or seems to prove — that it is rational to worry even about things that are statistically rare. The psychiatrist was sure his wife was crazy to even think of trying their house key on a neighbor's house. Yet the key opened the neighbor's door.

Though our executive function is smart, its thinking doesn't always match actual probability. For example, when flipping a coin, if it comes up heads seven times in a row, how likely is it that it will be tails next time? Most people would insist that it almost has to come up tails. Yet, statistically, the probability is still fifty-fifty. One way to explain the phenomenon is to say the coin has no memory. And since it has no memory of coming up heads seven times in a row, it doesn't know it should now come up tails.

So it is not irrational for the lawyer to believe he is at risk of being shot if he stays at the office the day following the gun incident. But ruminating about what might have happened triggers a barrage of stress hormones that impairs his ability to sense which mental processing mode he is in. Each disaster that goes through his mind — a combination of memory and imagination — triggers the release of stress hormones. If stress hormone levels rise high enough to disable reflective function — which ordinarily allows us to separate memory and imagination from what is real — what is in his mind has the same emotional impact as the event that actually took place.

The collapse of reflective function, whether it is due to excessive stress hormones, as in the lawyer's case, or to underdevelopment that makes reflective function excessively vulnerable to stress hormones, sets the stage for panic. Fears about what might happen solidify into a belief that it *is* happening. And, if we cannot see a way to escape from what we believe is happening, we panic.

CHAPTER 13

How Panic Is Triggered

A client emailed:

> *I have to sit in the exit row of a movie theater. Being a passenger in a car is troublesome. And church…well, forget that. Even sitting in the last row gives me anxiety. Any situation where I cannot escape, whether a physical barrier or a psychological barrier, is a no-go. And that's the crux of Captain Tom's program. He explains how it's not being able to escape that causes so much distress.*

As we have seen, humans have sophisticated systems to regulate arousal automatically and unconsciously. If these systems are not adequately developed, however, our emotional regulation may default to the mobilization system, which we expect will produce instant relief. Until escape has been accomplished, doubt that escape can be accomplished at all can cause panic.

Such concerns develop easily on the upper floor of a building, for example. Though escape is usually possible by walking down the stairs, that process takes time. When there is an urge to escape, if an exit is not directly in view, doubts may arise about how to leave the building. If these doubts lead to a state of alarm, doubt may be transformed into belief that escape is impossible. This, of course, means panic.

Once a person has experienced panic in a place where escape seemed impossible, being in that place — perhaps even thinking about being in that place — can trigger panic. Then panic can be triggered by being in any place where immediate escape is restricted. When the mobilization system does not instantly end the person's distress, the person may be pushed down into the immobilization response and freeze.

Why are some people more susceptible to this level of panic? The answer, once again, may lie in common early childhood experiences. It is not unusual for parents to put a baby to bed and let the baby "cry it out" without being comforted. Allan Schore has said that after a baby cries it out and appears to be asleep, the baby is actually in a frozen state of dissociated terror: in other words, in a state of immobilization. The trauma of being repeatedly forced into the immobilization system may cause this state to occur more readily in later life.

People who have experienced the involuntary immobilization response may come to fear the response itself, in certain situations or in any situation. For example, fear of becoming immobilized while escaping may stand in the way of attempting to escape. A woman who lived on the third floor of a converted Manhattan brownstone had only one way to exit her apartment: the original staircase inside the building. Warned that a fire could make the staircase unusable, she was advised to install a chain ladder that could be lowered from the window to provide an alternative escape route. She chose not to install it. Having had episodes of involuntary immobilization in the past, she believed she would not be able to use the ladder to escape. She was sure that if she began climbing down, she would freeze, lose her grip on the ladder, and fall to her death. She was convinced that even when facing the risk of death by fire, she would be unable to climb down the ladder. Though this may sound unbelievable to a person who has never experienced the immobilization response, it makes sense to a person who has.

Typically, a person who suffers from panic does not know that their advanced arousal-regulating systems are underdeveloped. They have no idea that such internal resources exist, much less that they are the source of automatic, unconscious regulation in other people. A person who panics doesn't understand why everyone else doesn't.

Perhaps surprisingly, some people who *do* have these resources don't know about them either. Since internal resources regulate automatically and unconsciously, people who are regulated by them are not aware that they are being regulated or how automatic regulation works. A person who doesn't panic doesn't understand why anyone else does.

Every childhood is different, but panic sufferers have one thing in common: they missed out on a caregiver-child relationship that allowed the development of unconscious regulation of arousal and automatic attenuation of alarm. Some know that their caregivers had problems with alcohol or other substances. Some have memories of family violence. But many people don't remember details that might explain what went wrong. Though their caregivers may have let them down, these people — even in adult life — do not understand how their caregiver-child relationship fell short of what they needed to enable them to independently regulate arousal.

Panic is not the panic sufferer's fault. Though every child should have a right to a well-developed internal replica system, this birthright is often not bestowed. For supportive internal replicas to develop, the young child must be consistently and appropriately responded to when hyperaroused. That means being responded to in a calm, attuned, and nonjudgmental way as a real person, as a separate person, and as a person with a right to their thoughts and feelings.

Therapy may help a person retrieve the details of their childhood. Ironically, one of my clients is a therapist who has specialized for years in the treatment of panic disorder. Though she was able to help her clients overcome their panic, she was unable to control her own. After she completed my fear-of-flying program, her intractable problem with panic disappeared both in the air and on the ground.

This client's own psychotherapy had illuminated the details of her childhood enough for her to identify what was lacking. I asked her to share some of her experiences with readers of this volume. Some of her experiences may throw light on your own.

I am currently a licensed psychologist who specializes in trauma, panic disorder, and PTSD. I train and publish nationally. I treat individuals, couples, and families. I have a general practice, though I have a focus on First Responders and the Deaf and Hard of Hearing. I climbed hundreds of mountains to get here, many on my hands and knees in desperation. I am not a victim. I am a learner. To understand how neuroscience helped and hindered me, I have to start at the beginning.

When I was a child, most would describe me as sensitive, gullible, shy, avoidant, obsessive, smart, funny, fearful, and a precocious kid. I started kindergarten at four years old, though I didn't want to. I remember the first day of school vividly and couldn't understand why my mother would leave me there alone with people I didn't know. I cried. She turned and left.

I recently lost my mother, who I cared for in her last year of life. My family had abandoned all responsibility for her care. They knew I would do it even if it was overwhelming for me, and it was. I cared for her and I'm glad I did. It turned out to be a gift to me.

My father died 23 years ago, or I don't think I could write this. I wouldn't want to hurt their feelings. I did and do love them both, but neither was taught or was equipped to be a parent. They did not, for whatever reason, hug, touch, or kiss us except on rare occasions. They did not provide verbal support, interest, words of affection, or "I love you," which my brothers and I needed to hear, which I learned later in life everyone needs to hear....

My grandmother, two aunts, a teacher in the 7th grade, though not seen often, were the only anchors I had. Luckily, they were enough to pull me through the craziness that was the house my parents built.

My therapist-client's childhood did not provide the well-attuned caregiving necessary for her to develop a robust internal replica system. Lacking resources within, she turned to others for calming. She had this to say:

Unconsciously I sought out people who were kind to me, supported me, or provided structure for me. I always had a good sense of humor, which I believed saved me on many occasions and also brought me a great group of friends who were always there for me. Still, I never told them what was happening in my house or in my body or mind. My household was very chaotic, loud, and without rules or stabilizing features that help children thrive.

Her parent-child relationships produced not stabilizing but destabilizing internal working models. These, stored in her internal replica system, obviously could not be used for emotional regulation. Moreover, her "loud" and "chaotic" home environment did not provide calming via her social engagement system.

Depending on another person for calming and regulation may have drawbacks. The relationship may have a price, such as being restricted, controlled, or abused by the other person. There are also pitfalls for the other person. They may find the relationship burdensome. And if they fail to provide regulation, they may be attacked verbally or even physically. In addition, if our early relationships have been traumatic, distrust may stand in the way of accepting the calming that others could provide.

I never told anyone what I was thinking or experiencing. I felt ashamed of these thoughts and feelings. Also, I didn't know that they were any different from what everyone one else was experiencing. I had a limited frame of reference. I didn't know I was pumping out stress hormones at every turn.

Though social engagement in my client-therapist's relationships outside the home got her by, they did not produce strong enough internal working models to carry over and enable her to regulate her emotions when she was alone. Without internal supports, her reflective function failed to separate imagination from reality. She was troubled by frightening things in her mind that did not exist in the real world.

The theories the teachers taught us became fodder for nightmares, day terrors, and obsessive fears. When it was explained to the class that the earth rotated and revolved around the sun, I had to hold on to my chair so I wouldn't throw up. The other kids continued pulling each other's hair and shooting spitballs. None were unnerved by this incredibly distressing and disorienting piece of information, if it were even true!

When imaginary threats trigger the release of stress hormones, imagination can seem real. My therapist-client continued:

I didn't have anyone who was stable, loving, and available on site who could provide guidance or modeling in emotional regulation or empathic attunement to help me manage what would become full-blown panic attacks and then agoraphobia. The agoraphobia led to my dropping out of high school. I was essentially trapped with little understanding of the cause and no idea of how to crawl my way out.

When executive function is unable to regulate arousal, the task is taken over by the mobilization system. For my client, mobilization did not work. She perceived threats inside, in her mind, as well as outside, in the world around her. She could not run away from them. So she retreated to her room, where the amygdala, exposed to fewer changes, released stress hormones less frequently. Nevertheless, her mind was active, and her imagined terrors still triggered the release of stress hormones.

> *While I knew nothing of the amygdala, I was almost constantly in a state of fear. My body buzzed with anxiety like an electric wire, my mind was on a loop playing over and over scenarios of death and destruction. I didn't know until adulthood that I had obsessive-compulsive disorder. Each year added a new fear or devastating catastrophe that could befall those I loved or harm that could come to myself.*

To a panic sufferer, this looks like a problem without a solution. But from my experience treating panic, I can say that the solution is simple. Stress hormones cause the urge to escape, but they may also make escape seem impossible. The problem vanishes when we prevent the release of stress hormones or override their effects.

We can inhibit the release of stress hormones by establishing a link between a situation known to cause panic, like getting into an elevator, and a memory that releases oxytocin. We can back that up with a link that overrides the effects of stress hormones, a link between a stressful situation and memory of the face, voice, and touch of a calming, attuned, nonjudgmental person.

But since panic can occur unexpectedly, in situations we have not encountered before, we need to cause unexpected arousal to activate the parasympathetic nervous system. These are, once again, the face, voice, and touch of a person who is both physically and emotionally safe to be with.

Since you can't depend on such a person to be there with you physically when you encounter a panic-inducing situation, you need to build that person into your memory so that they are always with you when you need them. You do this by remembering their face, voice, and touch.

To learn to counter unexpected hyperarousal, try the following practice. Instead of trying to control thoughts and events that could trigger panic, let them arise. Instead of trying to suppress feelings of being revved up, look for those feelings. Recognize stressful feelings at the very threshold of your ability to notice them, and immediately — before you do anything else — imagine that your calming person walks in, greets you, and comes over and gives you a hug.

Replay this scene in your imagination each time you feel even the slightest arousal. Each time you notice your heart beating faster, your breathing change, or a feeling of tension or flushing, imagine you see your friend come in, walk over to you, and give you a hug. It sounds too simple, doesn't it? But we are just adding the mental software needed to activate the parasympathetic nervous system you were born with. At around eighteen months of life, when something upset you, you anticipated relief. You imagined someone would respond. You imagined their face smiling at you, their voice reassuring you that everything would be all right, and their arms holding you until you felt calm. This is the way arousal becomes linked to relief. This is mental software that should have been given to you early in life. If it wasn't built in back then, pick this process and build it in now.

CHAPTER 14

Ending the Panic-Attack Domino Effect

A fear-of-flying client emailed the following:

When I was nineteen, I went to therapy to help with my agoraphobia. Afterward, I still had trouble with bridges and tunnels but could manage as long as traffic was moving. If traffic stopped on a bridge or in a tunnel it was all I could do to keep from jumping out of the car to get away. My heart would be pounding, my head spinning, my body in a cold sweat and shaking. More than once, when seeing traffic stopping on a bridge I have managed to get turned around to avoid it.

I truly felt my phobia was so severe I couldn't be cured. After all, it had been forty-one years. But since the SOAR program, I have been able to use the tools to stop the re-actions. For example, at the Sea Lion Caves on the Oregon coast, it's a two-minute ride in the elevator, a rickety one at that. Two minutes in an elevator is a long time.

In July I am planning another trip to Sweden and will be driving through an underwater tunnel two and a half miles long. I will be practicing the exercises to keep from panicking. If I can fly with help from SOAR I know I can handle a two-and-a-half-mile tunnel under water.

A panic attack has five typical elements: pounding heart, hyperventilation, perspiration, tension, and psychological changes. Panic generally starts with one of these elements. That element triggers a second, and the second triggers a third, and so on. For example, a pounding heart can cause tension; tension can cause hyperventilation, and so on, until we have what we call a full-blown panic attack.

To understand how we keep this domino effect from taking place, think of a strand of imitation pearls. If the string breaks, the beads go flying all over the place. But in a strand of real pearls, knots are placed between the individual pearls. Their purpose is to keep the delicate surfaces of the pearls from rubbing against each other. But the knot also serves another function: if the string breaks, only one pearl will come loose. Here is an exercise that works like those knots, separating and neutralizing each element of a panic attack so that no matter where panic starts, that is where it stops.

For many of us, emotional regulation depends on control and escape. So long as we are in control, we can make sure nothing upsets us. We regulate ourselves emotionally by controlling what happens. But if we lose control and things get out of hand, we need the possibility of escape as a backup to prevent panic. This is why panic is so easily triggered by what happens inside us. When we are frightened by a pounding heart, difficulty breathing, or psychological overwhelm, we can't get relief by running away.

Let's take a pounding heart as an example. Though this is not *in itself* a panic attack, it causes panic because we cannot control or run from a heart attack.

Similarly, hyperventilation is not *in itself* a panic attack, but it can induce panic if we are dependent on the mobilization system. Again, this is because we can neither control the situation nor run from it.

As to overwhelm, the mind continuously generates a sense of identity, of location, and of time. When the mind is overwhelmed, it can stop producing one or more of these anchors. Although anyone may feel overwhelmed on occasion, brief overwhelm is not traumatic. But protracted overwhelm can be terrifying, causing us to fear we are losing our mind.

Jet fighter pilots, who experience frequent, extreme mental demands, have a term for overwhelm: "being clanked." Think of a bell. If it is hanging free when struck, it rings clearly. But if it is held in the hand or otherwise constrained, it doesn't ring; it clanks. In the same way, when the mind has clarity, it is like a bell ringing clearly. When overwhelmed, it clanks.

Fighter pilots know overload is unavoidable. Since they also know that it is temporary, being clanked doesn't cause panic. If some mental ability drops out, they know it will always drop back in. But that knowledge is intellectual, and panic is emotional. Intellect may not control emotion.

To avoid relying on intellect, we use two tactics to neutralize each element of a panic attack. First, we link each element to a memory that activates vagal braking. This immediately overrides the stress hormones that drive the intense physical feelings and psychological changes of an incipient panic attack. Second, we link each element to a memory that stimulates the production of oxytocin. Oxytocin production ends the release of stress hormones. These links, once established, block the domino effect.

In the exercises I've developed to provide protective links and isolate the elements of panic, we use cartoon characters to illustrate the feelings. Cartoon characters help reduce the anxiety associated with the process because no matter what extreme difficulty they get into, we know they will always find a way out. There are no dead cartoon characters. Since we don't take their troubles too seriously, using them to represent intense feelings helps us do the linking exercise without stress.

On day 1, we link each element of a panic attack to a memory that applies the vagal brake. On day 2, we link each of the elements to an oxytocin-producing memory. On day 3, we go back to the links that produce vagal braking. On day 4, we return to linking each of the five elements to an oxytocin-producing memory, and so forth. In ten days, the links will be well established. By the way, if you have more than one oxytocin-producing memory or more than one vagal braking memory, use them — the more the better.

Establishing Vagal Braking Links

The release of stress hormones triggered by the amygdala prepares the mobilization system to run or fight by increasing our heart rate and breathing rate. If executive function identifies these physiological changes as normal, they do not cause concern. But in a person who equates arousal with danger, they may trigger the release of additional stress hormones. This in turn may cause reflective function — the cognitive capacity that allows us to determine what is real and what is imaginary — to be overwhelmed, allowing the physical changes to be experienced as life-threatening and cause panic.

To prevent panic, reflective function must remain viable under stress so that executive function can decide that these physiological changes do not signify danger. We keep reflective function viable by linking the physical manifestations of hyperarousal to a calming face, voice, and touch. Once these links are established, arousal activates the parasympathetic nervous system, and vagal braking overrides the stress hormones. The following exercises take you through this process for different elements of a panic attack.

Slowing a Rapid Heartbeat

The initial release of stress hormones causes a slight increase in heart rate. But if stress hormones build up, heart rate increases substantially, and the heart can be felt pounding in the chest. To control panic, you need to establish a link between this sensation and a person with whom you feel physically and emotionally safe.

To keep the thought of a pounding heart from causing anxiety, we'll visualize it happening to Clark Kent. He is confident that if anything goes wrong, he can turn into Superman and deal with it. But when he suddenly realizes he has lost the ability to become Superman because someone nearby possesses kryptonite (the substance that renders him powerless), his heart begins to pound. The cartoonist illustrates this feeling by drawing bold red exclamation marks on his chest and two slightly spaced curved lines alongside them to represent the chest expanding and contracting.

To establish a link between your pounding heart and your calming, attuned, nonjudgmental person, imagine that the person is holding the Clark Kent cartoon next to their face. Many of the calming signals come from a person's eyes and the area around the eyes. Next, since some calming signals are transmitted through the voice, remember the person's voice. Now imagine that the two of you are looking at the cartoon together and discussing Clark Kent's predicament. What is said is not important: focus on linking the calming characteristics of the person's voice to the pounding heart in the cartoon. In addition, some calming is physical, so establish a physical link. Imagine that while you talk about the cartoon, your friend gives you a reassuring touch or hug.

Easing Rapid Breathing and Difficulty Breathing

Stress hormone release causes a slight increase in breathing rate. Again, this is a natural response by the sympathetic nervous system to prepare the body for running or fighting, but it may be perceived as a threat in and of itself. This thought may trigger the release of additional stress hormones, leading to hyperventilation. If the additional stress hormones disable reflective function, the imagination of suffocation is experienced as real suffocation, and as a life-threatening situation that cannot be escaped. To prevent panic, we link hyperventilation to a calming face, voice, and touch.

Imagine Popeye the Sailor with his girlfriend, Olive Oyle. Popeye, being macho, doesn't want Olive to know he has panic attacks. Feeling anxious, he decides to fortify himself with his usual remedy, spinach. Reaching into his pocket, he finds it empty. No spinach! This is an emergency. Stress hormones push him to breathe faster. He breathes as fast as he can. Nevertheless, continued stress hormone release demands that he breathe faster. Since he can't, he gets the idea that he isn't getting enough air. As the stress hormones shut down his reflective function, imagination of suffocation is experienced as suffocation. To illustrate this, the cartoonist draws Popeye with his huge fist wrapped around his own long, skinny neck. Popeye starts to panic. Because he is tense, he inadvertently squeezes his own throat. He gasps, "Olive, I can't breathe!"

Again, imagine the calming person is holding the cartoon by their face. Now imagine a conversation about the cartoon as you look at it together. Then, as you talk, imagine the person giving you a reassuring touch.

Stopping Hot and Sweaty or Cold and Clammy Sensations

In preparation for running or fighting, we perspire, cooling the body before the anticipated exertion. If stress hormones build up, perspiration becomes sweating. As the sweat evaporates, we feel cold and clammy.

The SpongeBob SquarePants cartoon character is sometimes shown in panic, with sweat dripping from his face. Link this image to the face of the calming person. As you look at the cartoon together, imagine exchanging a few words about the cartoon. Then imagine receiving a calming, reassuring touch.

Releasing Tension

Stress hormones not only trigger the mobilization system, producing the urge to run or fight, but also activate executive function, which overrides the urge to run or to fight in order to assess the situation. The conflict between these two systems — run and don't run — causes tension in the body. The tension lasts until executive function commits to a plan to deal with the threat or determines that there is no threat.

Imagine Bruce Banner (the Hulk) becoming alarmed. He feels the urge to run, but his executive function holds him back. He starts turning green. His muscles tense and bulge. The buttons on his shirt are popping off. He is turning into the Hulk. Imagine that your calming person is holding this image by their face. Then, as the two of you look at the cartoon together, you exchange a few words. As you do, the person gives you a reassuring touch.

Preventing Psychological Changes

If stress hormones build up to high levels, psychological changes may take place, such as feeling unreal or surreal, dissociated or disoriented, or having a sense of looking at yourself from the outside. Other changes may include a loss of sense of self, of time, or of location. So far as I know, Scooby-Doo is the only cartoon character who demonstrates such changes. Imagine that Scooby-Doo's owner has left him in a kennel in some unfamiliar place. Alone and unable to escape, he starts to panic. As he does, he experiences psychological changes (the psychological changes you have noticed). To represent them, imagine that the cartoonist has drawn stars, exclamation marks, and spirals over Scooby's head. Link the cartoon of Scooby to your calming person's face. Then imagine looking at the cartoon together and talking briefly about Scooby's feelings. To establish a physical link to the calming person, imagine them giving you a calming touch.

Establishing Oxytocin-Producing Links

Once you've worked on using the cartoon images to activate vagal braking and override stress hormones, you can use them to practice preventing the release of those hormones in the first place, by producing a release of oxytocin instead. To do this, we'll link each element of high-level arousal, or a panic attack, to an oxytocin-producing memory. If the memory involves a person, imagine the person is holding the cartoon next to their face. Then, viewing the cartoon together, have a brief conversation, and share a sensual touch. If the oxytocin-producing situation is holding — or nursing — a baby, imagine someone is holding the cartoon close to the baby so you see the baby and the cartoon at the same time.

If the oxytocin-producing memory involves a pet, imagine the cartoon next to the pet's face, or hold the cartoon by your pet's face yourself. Next, establish a verbal link. Imagine talking to your pet about the cartoon. Follow that with a physical link, imagining touching the pet or perhaps receiving an affectionate lick or nuzzle.

We know from research that interacting with dogs can produce oxytocin. This is apparently because dogs look at their owners with complete devotion. What about cats? It depends on the cat. Some cats are affectionate, and others look at their owners as if to say, "What have you done for me lately?" If your cat is affectionate, linking to your cat will work.

Slowing a Rapid Heartbeat

First, establish a visual link between Clark Kent's pounding heart and an oxytocin-producing memory. Imagine that the person in the memory is holding the cartoon by their face. If the memory involves a baby or a pet, imagine you are holding the cartoon by the baby's or pet's face. To establish a verbal link, imagine the person speaking to you about experiencing a pounding heart, or imagine speaking to the baby or the pet as you view the cartoon. Finally, bring to mind physical touch as you visualize the cartoon.

Easing Rapid Breathing and Difficulty Breathing

Imagine the Popeye cartoon by the person's, the baby's, or the pet's face. Then imagine that the person speaks a few words as you look at the cartoon, or that you say a few words to the pet, about breathing. Next, recall a touch.

Stopping Hot and Sweaty or Cold and Clammy Sensations

Imagine the SpongeBob cartoon by the person's, the baby's, or the pet's face. Then imagine that the person says a few words to you, or you say a few words to your pet, about the feelings. And, with SpongeBob's feelings in mind, imagine a touch.

Releasing Tension

Imagine the cartoon of Bruce Banner turning into the Hulk. Imagine the cartoon by the face of the person, the baby, or the pet in your memory. Then, imagine hearing or saying a few words. Finally, imagine a touch.

Preventing Psychological Changes

Imagine Scooby-Doo starting to panic and feeling some psychological changes. A cartoonist would illustrate these by using stars, exclamation marks, and spirals over Scooby's head. Link the cartoon to the face. Then, looking at the cartoon together, imagine a few words about the cartoon. Then imagine a touch.

A word of caution is in order here. Certain medical conditions can cause symptoms similar to those of a panic attack. If you experience such symptoms, do not automatically assume that they are due to panic. A pounding heart, rapid breathing, feeling faint, or collapsing may indicate a serious physical condition. Anyone who experiences these symptoms should consult a qualified physician to determine whether a medical problem may exist.

CHAPTER 15

Alarm Attenuation

Imagine you are working on a project when the phone rings. Though you are deep in concentration, the ringing intrudes into your awareness and grabs your attention. When you answer the phone, the noise stops. If it didn't, having a conversation would be difficult, perhaps impossible.

We can think about the alarm system of the brain in a similar way. The amygdala monitors what goes on around you. It lacks the ability to know whether a change is important or not. So when it senses change, it refers the matter to executive function by releasing stress hormones. By causing alarm, the amygdala brings change to the attention of executive function.

Having seized executive function's attention, alarm must then relinquish its hold to enable executive function to operate. If alarm does not abate, reflective function cannot be focused inward to sense what kind of processing is going on: whether the amygdala is reacting to something perceived that needs to be dealt with, or something imagined that can be ignored.

In most people, alarm is automatically down-regulated, allowing executive function the calm it needs to do its job, but in panic sufferers it may not be. Without automatic down-regulation, executive function and reflective function are impaired. Reflective function failure allows imaginary threats to appear real. When that occurs, if escape seems impossible, panic may result.

We have seen how a child's expectation of a caregiver's face, voice, and touch can down-regulate hyperarousal. The same is true with alarm attenuation. When a child is alarmed, an attenuating sequence may take place, consisting of the following steps:

1. Alarm
2. Expectation of caregiver response
3. Imagination of the caregiver's face, voice, and touch
4. Activation of the parasympathetic nervous system and vagal braking

If reinforced, this sequence is installed in the child's unconscious procedural memory. Alarm attenuation developed during childhood remains active throughout the life span.

Though the relationship you had with your caregivers may have accomplished many good things, if you experience panic, most likely the relationship did not produce automatic calming. Only recently has it been understood that emotional regulation is relationship dependent and that the role of early caregivers, particularly the mother, is crucial. Allan Schore writes, "The child's first relationship, the one with the mother, acts as a template, as it permanently molds the individual's capacities to enter into all later emotional relationships. These early experiences shape the development of a unique personality, its adaptive capacities as well as its vulnerabilities."

Please understand that I am not blaming your caregivers. Their response to you when you were alarmed may have been based on how their own caregivers responded to them. Also, an inexperienced caregiver may not be able to respond calmly to a child's distress. Caregiver overreaction can transform a normal alarm experience into panic or terror. Peter Fonagy, an authority on child development, explains the process this way:

> If I was a little baby, and I feel anxious, I do not understand what that feeling is. And I look to my mom to make sense of it and my mom reflects, mirrors back to me a sense of anxiety, that will help me organize what I feel. If she exaggerates that and what she mirrors back to me is terror, then I will exaggerate my own experience of my constitutional self, my physiological reactions, and I will end up perhaps throughout my life exaggerating; I become one of those really anxious people who always at the slightest sign, at the slightest cue, will have a sense of panic or a sense of terror.

The importance of alarm attenuation is reflected in the procedure for dealing with an engine fire on an airplane. This is a serious threat that requires immediate attention. When training to deal with an engine fire, pilots not only memorize the procedure step by step, but they also practice these steps in a flight simulator until hands-on repetition establishes the procedure in their unconscious procedural memory, enabling them to carry it out even under extreme stress.

If the plane's sensors detect an engine fire, a large red warning light is illuminated on the instrument panel in front of the pilots, and a very loud alarm bell rings. The first step in the procedure is to press a button near the warning light that silences the bell.

It might seem that with an engine on fire, there would be something more important to do as a first step than turn off a bell. But no. Quieting the alarm in the cockpit — like down-regulating alarm in the mind — is the most important step in dealing with an emergency effectively and without mistakes.

One reason for this is that the bell is too loud for the pilots to hear each other. The noise must be silenced to allow them to work together on the problem that triggered the alarm. Here, the pilots play the role of reflective function, distinguishing real from imaginary threats. They need to determine whether the warning is due to a real fire or to a false alarm.

Experience has made it clear that in an emergency, pilots must work together in a very deliberate fashion to make sure no mistake is made. For example, a pilot hurrying through the procedure single-handedly could apply the engine fire procedure to the wrong engine. On a two-engined airliner, with one engine on fire and the other mistakenly shut down, the plane would be without power, and crash.

To avoid this, before shutting an engine down, the captain places a hand on the shutoff lever of the engine that has been identified as the problem. But before moving the lever, the captain must have the copilot's agreement that the captain's hand is on the correct lever. In other words, the copilot is the captain's backup reflective function.

Accidents have happened when the captain did not allow the copilot to play the role of reflective function before taking action. In fact, this was the cause of the worst crash in aviation history. At Tenerife, in the Canary Islands, on March 27, 1977, as the captain of a KLM 747 began to take off in foggy conditions, the copilot voiced concern that they had not been cleared for takeoff. The captain nevertheless continued with the takeoff. The KLM 747 collided with a Pan Am 747 already on the runway, resulting in 583 fatalities.

The way nature has designed us to deal with serious threats is similar to the warning system for an engine fire. When our sensor — the amygdala — detects a change, it releases stress hormones to alert or alarm us. Like the fire warning light and alarm bell in the cockpit, these neurochemical signals get our attention no matter what else we may be focused on. And, like the alarm bell, our feelings of alarm must be quieted if we are to think clearly enough to determine whether the danger is real.

If there is a real threat, executive function needs to determine a prudent course of action. And just as pilots can't work well together unless the alarm is silenced, executive function can't operate effectively if feelings of alarm continue. It takes one to two minutes for stress hormones to burn off enough for the sense of alarm to subside. In an emergency, that's too long to wait. Fortunately, alarm attenuation can override the effect of stress hormones and allow executive function to do its job.

Though you may not yet have developed general alarm attenuation, you may have developed automatic downregulation in a specific environment, perhaps one associated with a person whose presence made that environment secure. Identifying such a situation can increase your confidence that you can extend that sense of security to other situations. The following descriptions of experiences may help you find an example of your own.

When I was in Air Force pilot training, we completed our first thirty hours of flying in a relatively slow piston-engined plane, similar to those flown by amateur pilots. After thirty hours, we switched to a jet trainer. While I was flying the piston-engined trainer, other students flying the jet told us that an engine fire on the jet could cause it to explode. That, they said, was why it was equipped with an ejection seat, something our piston-engined plane did not have. This left those of us yet to fly the jet a bit uneasy.

On my first flight on the jet, as the plane was being flown by my instructor, I saw the red overheat light go on. This warning light indicates a situation just one step less serious than an engine fire. I looked at my instructor, who seemed oblivious to the red light. He just kept flying.

Although I was afraid we were facing a serious emergency, I was also afraid of incurring my flight instructor's wrath. As the seconds passed, my anxiety grew. Meanwhile, my instructor still seemed unaware of the red overheat light. Finally, I meekly pointed to it.

"False warning," he said. I looked at him quizzically. He pointed to the exhaust-gas temperature gauge. "Normal," he said. After the flight, he explained that the jet trainer was subject to false overheating warnings. If the warning had been valid, the exhaust gas temperature would have been considerably higher than normal.

The red warning light must have caused a release of stress hormones in my instructor. But his many years of experience in airplanes allowed him to calmly assess the situation and to determine that the red warning light was a false alarm. My instructor's measured response to the warning had an effect on me. The sense of safety I perceived in his face became linked to the warning light, as did the safety signals in the quality of his voice. Without being conscious of it, I had established what I now, in retrospect, could call "overheat-warning-light alarm attenuation."

Some years later, when I was in graduate school, my research partner and I became worried that we had entered answers from some questionnaires into the computer twice. If we had, our entire research project might have been ruined. We went to our professor and told him about our concerns. Both of us expected him to be extremely upset. Instead, he asked how far back were we sure our entries were correct. We told him we were sure everything was all right two days earlier. He picked up the phone, called the computer department, and told them to restore the research data stored the day prior to the possible errors.

Whatever stress the news of our mistake caused our professor was attenuated before it was even visible to us. He immediately came up with a solution. With the data restored from three days prior, we just resumed the data entry work from that point and thus could be sure there were no double entries.

Though alarm attenuation circuits are, for the most part, established during the formative years, later experiences such as these can strengthen those circuits or build new ones. We can observe the responses of role models and internalize them. Seeing how my flying instructor responded to the warning light provided situational calming: I internalized his response that this particular warning should be responded to calmly rather than reacted to as an emergency. This experience also provided me with general calming about warnings that might go off in the cockpit. I internalized his response that warning signals need to be responded to cognitively rather than emotionally.

Your alarm clock makes a noise to wake you up. When the alarm goes off, the dream that seemed so real a moment ago is dislodged, and reality takes over. When the annoying sound has done its job, you shut it off. In a similar way, once the amygdala has gained your attention with stress hormones that trigger feelings of alarm, those feelings have served their purpose. You now need to think clearly about the situation.

If you can think clearly, you determine — rather than imagine — what the amygdala is reacting to. If you can determine that what the amygdala is reacting to is no big deal, you can drop the matter and end the release of stress hormones. If you determine there is a problem, you can remain calm enough to weigh your options, choose a plan of action (or inaction), commit to your plan, and carry it out. But if you leave it to your imagination to identify the nature of the potential threat that the amygdala is reacting to, the action you take will be flawed.

At the moment of commitment to a plan, executive function tells the amygdala, "It's a done deal," and signals the amygdala to end the release of stress hormones. If you can't come up with a good plan, you may indeed decide that the best strategy is to escape the threat and run. There is a difference between *always* running away in response to unmitigated hyperarousal and *occasionally* running away because you have determined running to be the best strategy.

When calm, we look both outward at the world around

us and inward to critique and fine-tune our take on reality. Looking inward — employing reflective function — allows us to sense whether we are perceiving the world around us, remembering something from the past, or imagining. Under stress, however, we lose reflective function. And when that happens, we don't notice it. It's a catch-22: we would need reflective function to notice that reflective function isn't working.

If we are remembering or imagining something when reflective function shuts down, we begin experiencing it as though it were happening in the present. We do this every night. When we are asleep, reflective function is off duty, and whatever drifts into the mind — we call it dreaming — is experienced as real. If the dream is frightening, we call it a nightmare. When we wake up, our reflective function kicks in again. As it examines what was going on in the mind, we recognize that what we believed was real was a dream.

We can move into and out of a dreaming state even when wide awake, when stress hormones momentarily override reflective function. When the stress hormones subside and reflective function returns, we slip out of the waking dream, quite possibly never knowing we were in it. We may retain something we imagined, continuing to believe it is real when we unknowingly slide from the waking dream back to reality.

Trauma can cause flashbacks in which a past experience replays in the mind as though it were happening in the present. When a person is in a life-threatening, traumatic situation and escape is impossible, they may slide into immobilization. In this state, the brain is partially shut down and does not fully record what is taking place. If the memory of the event lacks time data, the memory may later be experienced as if were happening in the present. This can also happen when enough stress hormones are released to disable reflective function, even when the memory includes time data.

One or both of these factors may have played a role in the following example. In a Veterans Administration (VA) post-traumatic stress disorder training program for therapists, we were told about a client, a Vietnam veteran, who experienced a flashback while driving down the New Jersey Turnpike near Newark Airport. When a helicopter passed close overhead, he slammed on the brakes, stopped his car, and jumped into a ditch to escape enemy fire. The sound of the helicopter blades, associated with his experience in combat, may have triggered enough stress hormones to disable his reflective function. Or perhaps, when his memory of being under fire was formed, his mind was too overwhelmed to include time data.

Reflective function typically does not develop until around age three. Until then, children experience whatever is in their mind as real. Not only that, but children believe that everything in the world is in their mind. Fonagy terms this state of mind *psychic equivalence.*

Around this age, as we begin to observe our mental processing, we make an amazing discovery: some of the things in our mind do not exist anywhere else. This ability to look inward opens the door to a delightful new world: the world of pretend. Think of a four-year-old and a two-year-old playing together. The older child says, "Let's pretend we are in the jungle. There are lions and tigers. They are going to try to catch us and eat us. Look. There's one! He's after us! Run!"

The older child knows the predators are not real, but the

younger child is not yet sufficiently aware of his mental processing to understand this. To him, the imaginary lions and tigers are real. Terrified, he runs for his mother to save him.

When my daughter was very young, she told me she couldn't sleep because of a panther in the closet. I told her there was no panther. She was sure it was there. I searched the closet as she watched. I told her, "See? No panther." She nodded, but as soon as the door closed, she told me it was still there. She got out of bed and we searched the closet together. But when back in bed, she said, "It's still there." Finally — and I don't know where this idea came from — I said, "Would you like the panther to snuggle up with you in bed?" She smiled. "That would be fine," she replied.

To me, the panther was imaginary. To her, it was real. In the closet, it was threatening. In her arms, warm and cuddly, it became comforting. She fell asleep.

To produce an accurate take on reality, we need reflective function to monitor our thought processes and perform reality testing — an ongoing process of critiquing whether what is in the mind is, or is not, an accurate representation of what is outside the mind. If reflective function shuts down in response to a flood of stress hormones, this monitoring of our thought process stops. As we slip into a state of psychic equivalence, our mental functioning becomes that of a two-year-old. Whatever is in our mind — be it imagination, memory, or perception — is experienced as really happening. When imagination takes over, imaginary threats — like the panther in the closet — are experienced as real.

The disorder schizophrenia is a constant state of psychic equivalence in which the person does not recognize his thinking as his own processing, or his imagination as his own creation. Panic can result from a similar mental state.

Without automatic alarm attenuation to override the effects of stress hormones, reflective function collapses, and executive function cannot separate the imaginary from the real. If an imaginary threat is experienced as real and if the threat cannot be escaped, panic results.

In some cases, the strategy used to avoid an imaginary threat leads to problems. During my graduate school internship placement at a VA outpatient clinic, I was assigned to treat a young man who had been discharged from military service with a diagnosis of schizophrenia. His disorder came to light when he became physically ill. While sitting on a toilet, he imagined that a giant hand was reaching up from inside the toilet to grab him and pull him down through the drain into the sewer and drown him. He was unable to recognize that the hand was imaginary. Thus, his executive function was forced to deal with the imaginary hand as though it were real. Based on the information available to his executive function — that if he sat on the toilet, the hand could grab him — his executive function made a perfectly rational decision: avoid the toilet. After avoiding the toilet for two weeks, he became ill and was hospitalized. He explained his strategy for avoiding the life-threatening hand to his doctors. Trusting their reality testing over his, they diagnosed schizophrenia. He was discharged and sent to the VA for treatment.

To recover from schizophrenia, a person must understand that imagination can masquerade as reality. They must begin looking inward and questioning whether what they have in mind is real. My client lacked enough reflective function to examine what was in his mind and determine whether it was based on imagination or on perception. He continued to believe that his reality testing was superior to that of the doctors, and that the hand was real. He simply could not grasp the concept that he could put something into his own mind. Instead he insisted that someone else had put it there.

A panic sufferer has reflective function. But when stressed, it stops working, and then whatever is in the mind is experienced as real. So to avoid panic, you need to safeguard the operation of reflective function. Feeling the pounding of your heart, for example, is perception. But the idea that this pounding is a sure sign of a heart attack, though it springs from perception, is a thought. (You may never have thought of it this way, but a thought is a type of imagination.) Similarly, feeling short of breath is perception. It may lead to the idea that you are suffocating. If alarm about the thought is not attenuated, reflective function may fail, leading you to believe that you are actually suffocating. When stress hormone release causes alarm, unattenuated alarm can lead to terror that you are going crazy or dying.

To prevent panic in challenging situations, you need to recognize that the thought of being trapped in an elevator, for example, is not the same as actually being trapped in an elevator. You must learn that the thought of falling from a high place, though it may feel real while stress hormones race through your body, is still only a thought; it does not mean that you really are falling. Alarm attenuation helps protect reflective function so that you can tell the difference.

Alarm attenuation can be produced by the internal replica system. If that fails, attenuation reverts to the social engagement system. This requires the availability and responsiveness of a real person. If a real person is not available, or not adequately responsive, emotional regulation reverts to executive function. Executive function can provide alarm attenuation only if it has had enough previous experience with the perceived threat to recognize the threat as imaginary without the input of reflective function.

If executive function has no previous experience, and reflective function is not operative, imaginary threats may be experienced as real. The threat causes the release of additional stress hormones that further increase arousal. If executive function fails to regulate arousal, regulation reverts to the mobilization system, and the person seeks escape. If the person is able to escape, regulation takes place. If not, the person may slide involuntarily into immobilization and may panic, freeze, or faint.

Obviously, this downward slide needs to be stopped before it can start. Since activation of the parasympathetic nervous system is based on relationship, the answer is to build a relationship inside your mind that will activate the parasympathetic nervous system as needed.

CHAPTER 16

Establishing Automatic Alarm Attenuation

Alarm attenuation is vital. It keeps us from being overwhelmed, thus allowing us to think clearly enough to determine whether a threat is real or imaginary. If we determine that the threat is real, alarm attenuation enables us to down-regulate enough to develop a strategy to deal with the situation. If your capacity for alarm attenuation has not been fully developed, the exercises in this book can help.

You can establish automatic alarm attenuation by linking the feeling of alarm to the presence — or a replica of the presence — of an attuned and nonjudgmental person. As Stephen Porges explains, a person who is physically and emotionally safe to be with activates the parasympathetic nervous system. The person's face, voice, and touch unconsciously transmit signals that stimulate vagal braking, which overrides the effects of stress hormones. Since reception of these signals takes place outside consciousness, Porges refers to it not as *perception* but as *neuroception*. Neuroception of the person's safety signals activates your calming parasympathetic nervous system, slows your heart rate, and relaxes you. When this happens, you may feel your guard let down. Once you have linked feeling alarmed to a calming presence that enables you to override the effects of stress hormones, alarm attenuation takes place automatically.

Without alarm attenuation, once we become alarmed, we remain in that state until the stress hormones burn off. Extended alarm can trigger continued release of stress hormones and lead to high anxiety or panic. For example, I had a client who feared flying and felt alarmed even when seeing his digital clock read 737 or another airliner model number. His parents had been in a concentration camp during World War II. They taught him that survival depended on doing as one was told, not being noticed, and not asking questions. With his natural curiosity discouraged, his reflective function was also underdeveloped and subject to collapse under even moderate stress. Thus, the stress hormones produced by the sight of the number 737 were enough to shut down his reflective function and allow psychic equivalence to occur. Psychic equivalence is like a state of temporary schizophrenia. For this client, it made the thought of being trapped in a plane and plunging to the ground feel real and throw him into panic.

But the power of relationship is remarkable. He and I were able to find a memory that enabled him to avoid psychic equivalence, separate imagination from reality, and control panic. As a child, my client used to get into his father's Buick and go with him to Dunkin' Donuts. They had coffee and donuts together as his father smoked a cigarette. On these outings, his father was easygoing. My client experienced these moments with his father as moments of total acceptance. He recalled feeling his guard let down, which indicates full activation of the parasympathetic nervous system. We linked this memory of the Dunkin' Donuts visits to the feeling of alarm he experienced when thinking about flying. After he had reinforced this link, flying, even on long-haul flights to Europe, became not only possible for him, but comfortable. In addition, his related fears of bridges and tunnels disappeared. This outcome may seem amazing. But we humans are genetically programmed to feel safe when we receive calming signals from others. This capacity arose very early in human evolution. Though individuals may be able to survive independently, many human accomplishments have been possible only through cooperation. Other social animals, such as dogs and wolves that survive by hunting in packs, convey signals of cooperation through scent and behavioral signals, such as play fighting. In humans, signals that express cooperation come from the face, the voice, and body language.

We have already addressed how to link the five elements of panic to the presence of a calming person, and to various situations that cause alarm. Now we want to produce alarm attenuation, which enables us to prevent panic even in potentially alarming situations we haven't encountered before. We want a method of quickly and automatically triggering vagal braking to protect reflective function from the effects of stress hormones so that executive function can work properly.

Children develop the capacity for automatic alarm attenuation when arousal is consistently followed by calming. As an adult, you can still develop this capacity using the following two exercises. All you need is at least one memory of a moment when you received signals of physical and emotional safety.

The Three-Button Exercise

This is the exercise to use if you notice you are stressed about something. Remember a person with whom you felt your guard let down. The signals that cause your guard to let down are transmitted by the person's face, their voice, and their touch. I want you to imagine buttons you can press to calm yourself.

- Imagine your friend has pasted a sticker on their forehead bearing a picture of a button with the number 1 on it. Another sticker, showing button number 2, is pasted on their chin. A third sticker, with button number 3, is pasted on the back of their hand.
- Now imagine feeling alarmed.
- Imagine putting your finger on the button 1 sticker on their forehead and then releasing it. Their face comes clearly to mind. You see the softness in their eyes. It feels good.
- Imagine putting your finger on the button 2 sticker. As you release it, the person's lips begin to move, and you hear them greet you in a special way. You may notice that the quality of their voice calms you deep inside.
- Imagine touching the button 3 sticker on the back of their hand. When you release the button, the person lifts their hand and gives you a reassuring touch or a hug — whatever gesture is appropriate in your

relationship with this person. You may notice calming stillness rest on you.

You can activate vagal braking by pressing the buttons any time you wish. But we want to set up calming that works automatically. To establish automatic attenuation, intentionally remember feeling alarmed, and then press button 1. Remember the feeling again; press button 2. Bring the feeling to mind again; press button 3.

Now we'll fine-tune the exercise with steps that link the three buttons to the specific things you feel when highly aroused.

- Remember feeling your heart beat faster. Imagine pressing button 1 to bring to mind the memory of the person's calming face. This establishes a visual link between being aroused and then calmed by the softness of their face and gaze.
- As you remember feeling your heart beat faster, imagine you are pressing button 2 to hear a conversation you and your friend might have about that feeling. This links your increased heart rate to calming signals in your friend's voice.
- As you remember feeling your heart beat faster, pretend you are pressing button 3 to feel your friend's reassuring touch. This establishes a link between arousal and calming touch.
- Remember feeling your breathing get faster. Pressing button 1 brings to mind your friend's calming face to establish a visual link to that sensation.
- Next, establish a vocal link between rapid breathing and your friend's calming voice by pressing button 2.

Have a pretend conversation with your friend about your rapid breathing.

- As you notice your breathing, press button 3 and imagine the reassuring touch of your friend's hand.
- Recall starting to feel tense. Press button 1 as soon as you feel tension, bringing your friend's face to mind.
- Again, as you start to feel tense, press button 2 and imagine your friend is saying something to you.
- As soon you begin to feel tense, use button 3 to remember feeling your friend's calming touch.

Now, as an experiment, try a variation of the exercise using cartoon characters. This can reduce the anxiety associated with the exercise. We don't take it seriously when cartoon characters are distressed, because we know it will all work out in the end. Try it and see which version you prefer.

- Imagine the cartoon character's heart beat faster. Press button 1 and imagine that your friend is holding the cartoon by their face. As you see your friend's face and the cartoon, notice your friend's eyes.
- Imagine the cartoon character feeling their heart beat faster. Imagine you are pressing button 2 to hear a conversation you and your friend might have about the cartoon character's experience of that feeling.
- As you look at the cartoon with your friend, pretend you are pressing button 3 to feel your friend's reassuring touch.
- Imagine the cartoon character's breathing getting faster. Press button 1 and imagine your friend is holding the cartoon by their face to establish a visual link.

- Next, establish a vocal link between rapid breathing and your friend's calming voice by pressing button 2. Imagine a conversation with your friend about the cartoon character's rapid breathing.
- As you talk about the cartoon character's rapid breathing, press button 3 and imagine the touch of your friend's hand.
- Think of a cartoon character feeling tense. Press button 1. Bring your friend's face to mind. Imagine the cartoon by your friend's face.
- Press button 2 and imagine you and your friend are talking about the cartoon character's tension.
- As you and your friend have that conversation, use button 3 to bring to mind the feeling of your friend's calming touch.

The Alarm Attenuation Exercise

To produce completely automatic alarm attenuation, we train the mind to activate the parasympathetic nervous system automatically. Because the amygdala releases stress hormones every time it senses anything nonroutine or unexpected, we experience arousal several times a day. Link your actual feelings of arousal to your friend's face, voice, and touch. When feeling relief, we sometimes say, "ahh." Let each of those three letters remind you as follows:

- the letter "a": of their attuned face
- the first letter "h": of hearing their voice
- the second letter "h": of getting a hug.

Every time you sense arousal, imagine you see your friend walk into the room, come over to you, and give you a hug (or whatever form of touch is appropriate for your relationship). By imagining this in response to arousal or alarm, you cause the three elements that activate the parasympathetic nervous system — face, voice, and touch — to come immediately to mind.

Let your friend's presence linger in your mind for a minute or two. You could imagine your friend sitting down with you. You might imagine talking over what triggered you. Hanging out with your friend in this imagined way keeps the parasympathetic nervous system active until whatever stress hormones are present burn off.

In just a few days, bringing your friend's face, voice, and touch to mind each time you feel arousal will establish automatic alarm attenuation.

Tips

- Carry a photograph of the calming person. At work, keep it on your desk or wall. When you notice any level of arousal, glance at the photograph.
- When first noticing arousal, place your hand on the part of your body where you noticed the sensation of letting down your guard in your friend's presence. Picture the friend's face, remember their voice, recall their body language and their calming and reassuring touch. The touch of your own hand becomes linked to your friend's calming presence.
- If it isn't easy for you to bring the calming person's face to mind, just imagine their touch. Instead of visualizing that person coming into the room, pretend

that the person is always with you, standing right behind you. When you feel stressed, imagine feeling the person's arms reaching around you and giving you a hug. Imagine that you don't even have to ask: they just do it when you need it.

- If possible, make an arrangement with the calming friend that you can call or text them when you feel arousal. You don't necessarily need a reply. Just knowing that your friend has you in mind is enough.

It's never too late to establish automatic alarm attenuation. One of my clients, at the age of seventy-eight, had never flown because of panic attacks. A therapist himself, he had tried every form of therapy to control panic. Each of them helped some, but until he tried this method, panic persisted.

He was born prematurely in a remote area in the Virginia mountains. The attending physician, seeing how premature he was, was sure he would not survive and set him aside in order to care for the mother. After his difficult birth, he also had a difficult early childhood. His mother was frail. When she became unable to lift him, she left him in his playpen all day, even when changing his diaper. When he grew too big for the playpen, she tied him by his leg to the kitchen table. When his father came home, his parents fought in the kitchen. Tied to the kitchen table, he had no way to escape the tensions. Feelings of arousal became strongly associated with danger.

His first panic attack came when he was eight years old. He said, "I didn't know what was happening. My mom just knew something was going on." Looking back, he says,

"Abandonment feelings I had as a child affected me. I'm not in that situation now, and can use the tools I have in my toolbox."

He took his first flight free of panic. While away, he ventured out into the Atlantic on a whale-watching excursion. After learning how to prevent in-flight panic, he found he could also control panic on the ground. "I had help from several sources. Every source helped some. But nothing resolved it completely until I shut down the amygdala. I am just amazed at the effect that has had. It is just a wonderful treatment."

If freedom from panic has eluded you for years, there is good reason to be gentle with yourself. You deserve no blame. After all, this person is a therapist and a minister. He has two PhDs, one in psychology and one in theology. With all that knowledge and life experience, he did not find freedom from panic until he was seventy-eight years old. It's never too late.

CHAPTER 17

Your Manual Backup
to Control Panic

"What if this doesn't work?" I hear this question about automatic control repeatedly from clients when they are facing a situation in which they previously experienced panic. Though automatic alarm attenuation works, nothing can keep you from imagining that it won't. You may feel better if you have another process to fall back on.

Here's an email from a person who had not yet learned automatic control. She found that the exercise described in this chapter gave her good conscious control. "I have experienced panic for some twenty-five years now," she told me. "When I feel it coming on, I do the 5-4-3-2-1 exercise and it really helps to stave it off. It is really helpful for bringing me back from the edge before I get there."

This backup is a mind game that takes your full concentration, keeping anxiety-producing thoughts out of your mind for two minutes or so. That's long enough for accumulated stress hormones to burn off and provide you with a window of opportunity to focus your mind as *you* choose.

Since this exercise is a form of distraction, use it only as a backup, not as a first line of defense against anxiety or panic. If used as your primary defense, distraction can prevent the development of automatic control.

The 5-4-3-2-1 Exercise

Focus on an object in front of you. Keep your focus on that object throughout the exercise. If your focus drifts, just bring it back.

Say, "I see," and name something in your peripheral vision. Say, "I see" and name something else in your peripheral vision. Continue until you have made five statements. For example, "I see the lamp, I see the table, I see a spot on the lampshade, I see a book on the table, I see a picture on the table."

Say, "I hear" and name something you hear. Repeat this statement another four times. If you can't detect five different sounds, repeat some.

Say, "I feel" and name an external sensation (not internal, like your heart pounding or tension). Continue until you have made five statements. For example, "I feel the chair under me, I feel my arm against my leg," and so on.

This set of statements makes up one cycle. Paying close attention to sights, sounds, and sensations takes intense concentration, which is exactly what you want. As you concentrate on these nonthreatening things, your jolt of stress hormones burns off, and you relax. You don't have to *force* yourself to relax; it happens naturally.

That completes the first set of statements. Now,

repeat the process, but instead of making five statements, make four. If you need to repeat the process again to calm yourself, make three statements, and so on down to one, if necessary. The reason for varying the number is to sustain your concentration. If you simply repeated the exercise without variation, you would soon be able to do it without much thought. Your mind might be able to entertain anxiety-producing thoughts while you worked through the exercise. With a varying number of statements, the exercise remains complex enough to require all your concentration.

After you have finished the exercise, if you want to be even more relaxed, or to fall asleep, do the exercise again starting with five statements. If you lose count, that is a good sign — it means you are relaxed. There is a video of this exercise at: www.fearofflying.com/free-video/5-4-3-2-1-exercise.shtml

If any of the other exercises described in the book fail to calm you enough, use this backup exercise to burn off the stress hormones and focus your mind where you, rather than the stress hormones, want to focus it. But to encourage the development of automatic alarm attenuation, take a minute before you do the 5-4-3-2-1 exercise to write down what triggered your anxiety. Later, break the trigger down. Separate it into its parts. Before facing that situation again, use the exercises in previous chapters to link each part of the triggering event to a friend's face, voice, and touch, and to a memory that releases oxytocin.

CHAPTER 18

Strengthening Executive Function and Reflective Function

An engineer asked why feelings overtake his ability to think logically:

> I have a rational, logical thinking mind 99.99 percent of the time. I understand how to take in my surroundings and know I'm safe. But my emotions get a hold of me and make me think something awful will happen.

Ordinarily, reflective function allows us to distinguish among perception, memory, and imagination. But when stress hormones build up, reflective function stops detecting which kind of mental processing is going on. We experience whatever is going on in our mind as if it were real. Past or imagined events seem to be happening in the present, or about to happen.

If reflective function is well developed, it falters only when stress hormone levels are very high. But, according to Peter Fonagy, robust reflective function is a "hard-won developmental acquisition" that "grows out of interpersonal experience." A caregiver who tunes in to a child's inner experience teaches and encourages the child to do the same.

Some professions demand continued development of reflective function. I'll give you a personal example. At about ten months into my US Air Force flight training, I began learning to fly using instruments. Pilots need to learn to navigate using instruments rather than just visual information because in darkness or fog, the ground is not visible. My instructor sat in the front seat of the jet trainer. I sat in the back under a tent-like hood that allowed me to see only the plane's instruments. The outside world was blocked from view, as it would be when flying in clouds or fog.

One training flight is deeply etched in my mind. My instructor set up a simulated approach to the airport runway. Using the instruments, I produced a mental picture of the plane's location relative to the runway. I was confident that I was on the proper path to land on the runway. My instructor asked, "How are you doing?"

"Fine," I replied.

"Are you sure?" he said. I assured him that I was.

"I've got the plane," he said, taking over the controls. "You come out from under the hood." I had no idea what he was driving at. When I removed the hood, I saw the airport was nowhere in sight. Worse, we were flying alongside a highway, and the tops of the telephone poles were higher than the plane. I had mistakenly — but with complete confidence — almost flown the plane into the ground. Had this been a real instrument landing, I would have crashed within seconds.

My instructor didn't say another word. He didn't need

to. He knew that I was shocked by the contradiction between my mental picture of the plane's position and reality. This experience led me to develop the kind of mental discipline needed to fly safely: to question every thought for accuracy before acting on it.

Reflective function is your internal flight instructor: it scrutinizes your take on reality, checks it for errors, examines what you plan to do, and critiques you as you do it.

The Need to Be Right

Sometimes, even if our reflective function is well developed, we ignore or overrule it. One cause of this tendency is the emotional need to be right about things. During a car race at a park in Ponca City, Oklahoma, as I was going around a left-hand curve at maximum speed, an awareness crept into my mind that the right front tire was going to brush the edge of the pavement. Instead of making a correction, I thought, "No, you're right."

Reality was about to show me otherwise. To go around a curve at maximum speed, a race car needs all the adhesion with the road surface that the tires can produce. If even 1 percent of adhesion is lost, the car may slide out of control. The tire did indeed brush the pavement edge, causing a loss of adhesion. The car slipped off the pavement onto the dirt shoulder. I turned the wheel sharply left to head the car back onto the pavement. It shot all the way across the pavement before I could make another correction. Suddenly, at sixty or seventy miles per hour, I found myself steering around trees.

In such a situation, there is no conscious thought; just action and reaction. Amazingly, I found myself back on the roadway, and I won the race in spite of my excursion through the woods. Instead of feeling like a winner, though, I realized I had been very stupid to let my ego overrule the awareness my reflective function had given me that there was a correction I needed to make.

Years later, I told a psychiatrist friend that I question every thought and every potential action. He was shocked. He said, "What a terrible burden!"

"No," I said. "You have to do that as a pilot. If you don't question everything, you will not survive. It isn't a burden; it is just a way of life." In aviation, there is a saying: "There are old pilots, and there are bold pilots, but there are no old, bold pilots."

The more we critique our thinking, the stronger our reflective function becomes. And the less we do so, the weaker our reflective function becomes, and the more vulnerable to collapse in moments of stress.

We don't notice when we slide into psychic equivalence. We have no awareness of the distortions in our thinking that others find obvious. We believe we are absolutely right.

Representing Reality in the Mind

Freud proposed a distinction between what he called *psychic reality* and *factual reality*. Psychic reality is a person's take on reality that has not been subjected to verification. Factual reality is a disciplined, self-examined mental representation of reality, perhaps cross-checked with others for accuracy. We can be resistant to questioning and examining our take on reality to develop an accurate mental representation. We may prefer just to believe we are right. Perhaps you've heard the phrase "Often wrong, never in doubt."

Relying on psychic reality goes hand in hand with weak reflective function and psychic equivalence that produces unjustified certainty. Freud wrote, "What characterizes neurotics is that they prefer psychical to factual reality, and react just as seriously to thoughts as normal people do to realities." He was describing the phenomenon we now call psychic equivalence.

Preference for psychic over factual reality is not new. Plato addressed this tendency 2,400 years ago in his famous allegory of the cave. Plato's mentor, Socrates, described a hypothetical cave in which prisoners were chained facing a blank wall for their entire lives. All they could see of the world were shadows cast on the wall. A prisoner who escaped from the cave would discover the sun, observe objects in the sunlight, and realize that the shadows he had regarded as the whole of reality were mere artifacts of light being blocked by objects.

If the prisoner returned to the cave, his fellows would not believe that his excursion had given him greater understanding of reality; rather they would think that it had blinded him. "Men would say of him that up he went and down he came without his eyes; and that it was better not even to think of ascending; and if anyone tried to loose another and lead him up to the light, let them only catch the offender, and they would put him to death."

Freud regarded a preference for psychic reality as neurosis, his term for mental illness. I see it as fitting with a limited ability or inclination to reflect on and critique our own thought processes. A weak reflective function, as we have seen, can result in psychic equivalence that allows imaginary fears to seem real and cause panic. But the opposite can also be true. A person can be comforted by the certainty produced by psychic equivalence: instead of imagining disaster and becoming certain of it, they imagine divine protection and are certain of it. Belief that one is protected in this way can control anxiety — but only, of course, if there is no doubt. A person who has been panic free can become unexpectedly subject to panic if their certainty of safety is fractured by doubt.

Fonagy suggests that people with good self-esteem may have as many negative thoughts about themselves as people with poor self-esteem. The difference in self-esteem levels may be due to psychic equivalence. "They experience ordinary negative self-evaluations (which we all have) in a psychic equivalent mode and they feel these thoughts with the full force of reality." When a negative self-image comes to mind, it triggers stress hormones. If reflective function is weak, psychic equivalence causes the person to accept the negative thought as though it were a fact. A person not prone to psychic equivalence would regard the thought as merely a thought.

If we apply this dynamic to panic, we can see that an anxious person may have no more catastrophic thoughts than a confident person. The pivotal difference may be the strength of their reflective function. When rapid heartbeat causes the catastrophic thought "What if I'm having a heart attack?," stress hormones are released. If reflective function is strong enough to withstand the stress hormones released by the thought, the person recognizes the thought as conjecture. If reflective function is not strong enough, it collapses, and psychic equivalence causes the thought to be experienced as fact. Though catastrophic thinking is said to be more common in anxiety-prone persons, it may only *seem* more prevalent because such people take catastrophic thoughts more seriously.

Reflective function can be strengthened and made less vulnerable to disruption by stress hormones. This requires ongoing discipline, consistently reminding yourself that your thinking is fallible. But don't worry. Everyone's thinking is fallible. The person who recognizes that fact is ahead of someone who does not.

Inner Awareness

Reflective function, our ability to look inward, is strengthened by the willingness to accept what looking inward reveals. We all have unwanted thoughts and feelings. What do we do about them? Do we make room for them, or do we try to block certain feelings from awareness?

It is impossible to place precise limits on our awareness. To keep a certain thought out of mind, we have to remember not to think about it. This, of course, keeps us aware of what we are trying to be aware of. So, since the unwanted thoughts and feelings are inside, we attempt to stay focused on what is outside.

If this is a strategy you have been using, it is not surprising that you have panic attacks. When you avoid inner awareness, you arrest the development of your reflective function, preventing it from growing strong enough to stand up to stress hormones.

You've probably guessed I'm going to tell you to make a 180-degree turn. You need to make room in your awareness for things you would rather not be aware of. You can make some progress in this effort through mental exercises such as yoga or meditation, but only if you practice them in a form that widens your awareness rather than focusing on one thing. For example, meditation focusing on the breath is a distraction, a form of escape. Though practitioners may tell you it will bring you peace, it will not. It is an attempt to find peace through escape. Just as a person with anxiety may seek peace by never leaving their home, the person who focuses on breathing finds no lasting peace. These forms of meditation close your awareness. To deal with anxiety, you want to practice a form of mental exercise in which you allow thoughts and feelings to enter your awareness freely, with acceptance.

A person may try to escape inner awareness in other ways, such as by using alcohol or other drugs. A workaholic avoids unwanted thoughts by staying busy at work. The form of escape that is hardest to recognize is the diversified one. The person stays focused on one activity for a while, then switches to a different one. Staying fully absorbed in a series of activities that you control blocks unwanted thoughts from coming into your awareness.

Avoiding inner awareness keeps a person from developing the reflective function needed to avoid panic. It also creates a second problem: when something you have successfully kept out of mind suddenly breaks through and comes into your awareness, it can cause panic.

My father was an athletic coach. Athletic training and competition involve physical discomfort and pain. He taught us to avoid awareness of discomfort and pain by focusing on the game. That works, but only up to a point. If the pain suddenly breaks through, it can be shocking.

As I began jogging one morning, I felt a slight pain in my ankle. On a scale from 0 to 10, it was a 1. After a few more strides, it went to a 2 and then to a 3. As I continued running, the pain continued to increase. Gradually, it became quite intense, a 7 out of 10. Nevertheless, since I maintained awareness of the pain, and since it increased only gradually, I simply adjusted. Shortly after it reached a 7, it began to lessen. Within a few minutes, it had disappeared, and I was able to continue my run as planned.

If I had used my father's strategy to deal with this pain, I would have had a problem. Let's say I had the ability to block pain up to level 5 by focusing on jogging. As I began jogging, I would have blocked the pain when at levels 1 through 4. Even when it reached a 5, I would have been unaware of it.

But when the pain reached a 6, it would have broken through my ability to block awareness. After several minutes of jogging with no discomfort at all, I suddenly and unexpectedly would have been hit by the pain. I might have thought, "Wow. I had no pain at all, and suddenly this. I must have broken something." That would have been shocking. My amygdala would have reacted to the unexpected pain; it would also have reacted to the idea of being injured. With a double release of stress hormones, I might have gone into psychic equivalence, the state in which I believed I really had broken a bone. The idea of having sustained a serious injury would be accepted as fact. I would have stopped jogging. I might even have sat down and waited for someone to come by and call for medical help.

Avoiding awareness causes trouble. When awareness is avoided, body awareness is avoided, and we ignore the early signs of stress. Finally, when the stress builds up to the point that it breaks into our awareness, it is at such a high level that it startles us.

Dr. Lori Haase and a team of researchers at the University of California, San Diego, found that people who maintain body awareness are better able to adapt positively to stress.

Self-Examination

Disciplined self-examination may be uncomfortable. Looking inward may reveal things we would rather not be aware of. It may disturb our peace of mind as conflicts ordinarily kept out of mind come into awareness. In time, perhaps with the aid of a therapist, looking inward can become more comfortable and allow us to enjoy the companionship of our inner self.

A person with schizophrenia is more likely to recover if they can look inward and recognize that what they experienced during a schizophrenic state was imagination. For example, they may be able to recognize that the voice they believed came from some other person was generated by their own imagination but that, in the absence of reflective function, psychic equivalence made the voice seem real. Similarly, a person who has had episodes of psychic equivalence due to stress is more likely to strengthen their reflective function if they come to recognize that what they experienced as real when under great stress was really imagination.

Look back. Recall a time of stress when something imaginary seemed real, something you were certain was going to happen did not eventuate, or something that seemed like fact turned out to be false. Though you could not use your reflective function at that time, you can do it now. Reflect on the event and examine why you clung to your initial, erroneous take on the situation. Questioning and critiquing your past thinking now, when you are not stressed, can strengthen your capacity to challenge flawed thinking and psychic equivalence when you are under stress in the future. The ultimate goal is for reflective function to sense the potential onset of psychic equivalence quickly enough to shut it down. The following exercise can help you develop this ability.

Imagination or Perception Exercise

This exercise can help you become more aware of which type of mental processing you are doing at any given time. It will show you how easy it is to slide from perception into memory. There is nothing inherently wrong with that shift: the object of the exercise is to become aware of it.

Traveling down a road, name out loud the things you see. While you are doing this, your mental process might go like this: "Yellow school bus. Telephone pole. Road sign. Billboard. White line. No-passing markings. Red Ford. (Huh, that's like the one I took Mary Sue to the beach in. She looked nice in her bathing suit. I liked her smile.)"

In this example, the last words said out loud are "Red Ford." The association between the red Ford and Mary Sue takes you into memory, and you go silent. Going silent is your clue that you have switched mental processing modes. As you continue the exercise, notice when you feel a pull to stop speaking. You may hesitate and catch yourself as you slip from perception toward memory.

Front Door, Back Door

When we are calm, it is easy to separate imagination from perception. But when we are stressed, reflective function collapses, and we lose our ability to distinguish the imaginary from the real. This cannot happen while we are able to sense which mental process is active: imagination or perception.

If you encounter a snake in the woods, an image of the snake is transmitted from the retina of your eye to the amygdala, and you freeze in your tracks instantaneously, without consciously knowing why. One-tenth of a second later, the image in the retina has been processed, allowing you to see the snake. Your amygdala protected you from the snake before you were able to see it or think about it.

Perception can release stress hormones before we are consciously aware of a threat. With imagination, stress hormones are released *after* awareness. If you feel a jolt of stress hormones before knowing why, you are dealing with perception. If you feel it after a disturbing thought, you are dealing with imagination. Feelings caused by thinking are evidence not of what is in the real world around you, but only of what is in your mind. Before accepting that "feeling is believing," look for substantial evidence.

The following visualization can help you develop this ability. Think of your amygdala as having a front door and a back door. Since the amygdala sits behind the eyes, you can think of information from the eyes as entering the amygdala through the front door. By contrast, imagination, formed in the "mind's eye," enters the amygdala through the back door.

As you go through your day, look inward now and then. Ask yourself, what is in your mind? Did it come in the front door, from what you see? Or did it come in from the back door, from your imagination?

Accepting Inner Conflict

Once you have developed your capacity for alarm attenuation and it is protecting your reflective function and keeping it active, you may notice a problem. Reflective function looks inward. Although this is necessary to prevent psychic equivalence, it also leads to awareness of inner conflicts, and this can be distressing.

For years, I wished I could avoid inner awareness. It meant awareness of disturbing thoughts, guilt, and a gnawing awareness of mistakes. It seemed to me that if I could avoid looking inward, I would stop seeing the conflicts that plagued me.

It never occurred to me that conflict could be something we are *supposed* to be aware of. I envied people who did whatever they felt like doing at any given moment. But when I went into therapy, my therapist told me that the people I envied lacked a fully developed self. She pointed out that a person who does whatever they feel like doing often makes a mess of things. She explained that though being aware of conflict is uncomfortable, grappling with conflict can help us reach goals, experience satisfaction, and avoid regret.

In her words, "The hallmark of mental health is the ability to tolerate ambiguity." Now as a therapist myself, I better understand what she was trying to say. We are multifaceted. Since our different facets have different aims, conflict is inevitable.

We need to bring conflict into awareness, where we can develop a compromise between different facets of the self that is in the best interest of the whole self. If conflicting interests are not made conscious, we satisfy the desire that is strongest at the moment. After that desire is discharged by action, there is a period of satisfaction. Then a conflicting desire comes to mind. "Why did I do that, when I really want to do this?" Or, "Why did I buy that one? I hate it. I wish I had bought the other one." With inner awareness, conflicts play out and reach an agreed-upon compromise that can be adhered to.

The very personal journey from avoiding awareness of certain aspects of oneself to acceptance is not easy. Completion will likely require the help of a therapist. But, when these facets of the self are revealed rather than obscured, the payoff, in terms of life satisfaction, is enormous. When the various facets negotiate, compromise, and settle on workable goals, it becomes possible to steer a steady course rather than an erratic one.

Part IV

Your Ten-Day Plan to End Panic and Claustrophobia Forever

CHAPTER 19

Step-by-Step Instructions

You already know that arousal needs to be controlled auto-matically and unconsciously. When it isn't, panic can result. This chapter outlines the ten-day plan to increase automatic regulation and to reduce stress hormone release to end panic.

- To reduce excessive up-regulation, we link an oxytocin-producing memory to each situation that triggers us.
- To increase down-regulation, we link stressful situations to a calming friend's face, voice, and touch.
- To increase automatic alarm attenuation, we program unconscious procedural memory to initiate calming whenever we become hyperaroused.

We start by going back to chapter 6. When stimulated, the vagus nerve overrides stress hormones. It slows the heart rate and relaxes other body organs. It is the active component of our calming system, the parasympathetic nervous system. To put this understanding into practice, on day 1 of the plan, we link vagal braking to the anxiety-provoking experience of riding in an elevator. Next day, we link it to a different anxiety-provoking situation of your choice. For the next two days, we shift our attention from overriding stress hormones to preventing their release. Then for two days we focus on ending the panic-attack domino effect. Days 7–9 are devoted to the important work of establishing alarm attenuation. On day 10, we just go through the day and see how we are doing, to check out — and enjoy — the results.

Day 1

1. Reread chapter 6, "Control Panic and Claustrophobia with Vagal Braking."
2. Remember a person with whom you felt your guard let down.
3. Link the person's face, voice, and touch to each step of the elevator exercise in chapter 6.

Day 2

1. Reread chapter 7, "Control Panic and Claustrophobia with Oxytocin."
2. Identify an oxytocin-producing memory.
3. Link the oxytocin-producing memory to each step of the elevator exercise.

Day 3

1. Identify a different situation that tends to trigger panic.
2. List the events that take place in that situation.
3. Link the memory of the person's face, voice, and touch to each event in the sequence.

Day 4

1. Continue with day 3 situation.
2. Use the day 3 list of events.
3. Link an oxytocin-producing memory to each event in the list.

Day 5

1. Reread chapter 14, "Ending the Panic-Attack Domino Effect."
2. Remember a person with whom you felt your guard let down.
3. Link the memory of the person's face, voice, and touch to each of the five elements of a panic attack.

Day 6

1. Refer to chapter 14, "Ending the Panic-Attack Domino Effect."
2. Identify an oxytocin-producing memory.
3. Link the oxytocin-producing memory to each panic element.

Day 7

1. Reread chapter 16, "Establishing Automatic Alarm Attenuation."
2. Do the Three-Button Exercise.

Day 8

1. Refer to chapter 16, "Establishing Automatic Alarm Attenuation."
2. Do the Three-Button Exercise and the Alarm Attenuation Exercise.

Day 9

1. Refer to chapter 16, "Establishing Automatic Alarm Attenuation."
2. Do the Three-Button Exercise and the Alarm Attenuation Exercise.

Day 10

1. Put the exercises behind you. Just go about your day.
2. Confirm that alarm attenuation is active and is being done in the background.
3. If you feel anxiety, alarm, or panic, identify its trigger. Write it down. At the end of the day, link the trigger to an oxytocin-producing memory and to a vagal-braking memory.

CHAPTER 20

Nine Questions about Your Ten-Day Plan

1. How long does it take to do the linking exercise one time?

Clients tell me it takes them about twenty minutes.

2. Should you do the exercises with a therapist, or by yourself?

You can do the linking exercises with a therapist, on your own, or both. The presence of an attuned, nonjudgmental person activates the calming parasympathetic nervous system. Not all therapists fit the bill. Some therapists are trained to offer advice. Some are taught to avoid discussions about their own experience. But some are taught that the most important thing a therapist can do is to relate to clients in a nonjudgmental, person-to-person way.

A related question is whether you should choose your therapist as the calming person to link your emotional challenges to. If you feel your guard let down while talking with your therapist, they may be just the right person to link to. You can ask your therapist to go through the linking exercise with you. Or you can simply link a troubling memory to a memory of being with your therapist at a time when you felt your guard let down.

3. Should you relax before doing the exercises?

Yes. I would like you to have a stress-free, anxiety-free experience with these exercises. If you're subject to troubling thoughts and memories while attempting the exercises, doing the 5-4-3-2-1 exercise beforehand is a useful way to dump the stress hormones that keep that vicious cycle going.

And why not relax? Is there any good reason to stay all tensed up? Well, there is a common but irrational one. When calamity has taken place "out of the blue," we are shocked by the realization that some meaningless random event could end our life. For relief, we may turn to magical thinking. The belief that everything happens for a reason offers us the illusion of control. For example, if we believe calamity is punishment for wrongdoings, we seek to control calamity by avoiding sin. Or, if we believe lack of worry causes bad things to happen, we worry to avoid tempting fate.

If you can see through the myth that expectation of disaster helps prevent it, maybe that will allow you to take the risk of relaxing. But if that is too big a risk, consider choosing to worry just enough. Pick a specific thing to worry about, and worry about only that. Or set aside a specified few minutes once a day to worry.

4. Should the linking exercise be done with eyes open or closed?

Either works. Try both and see which you prefer.

5. What if I feel like it isn't working?

The only way to tell whether this process is working is to test it in real, potentially panic-inducing situations. These exercises are designed to program your unconscious procedural memory, as is done when training emergency room staff, pilots, and first responders, so that you can always access the steps when you need them, without your even having to think about it. Your unconscious procedural memory performs for you when your conscious mind can't. If you're asking this question because you are imagining situations where the process *won't* work when you need it, don't let your imagination deceive you or stop you from giving it a try.

6. What if your unconscious procedural memory doesn't kick in?

When your mind drifts off your driving occasionally, does your car drift off the road? No. When it comes down to brass tacks, your unconscious mind is a lot more capable than your conscious mind. If you have linked to a memory that provides vagal braking, your parasympathetic nervous system will override the effects of stress hormones. If you have linked to a memory that produces oxytocin, your amygdala will not release stress hormones in the first place. So the only questions are these: Have you identified a moment when you felt your guard let down, and done the exercise to establish links to the challenging situation and to the feelings associated with arousal? And have you identified a moment when you produced oxytocin and done the exercise to link that memory to feelings of arousal? If so, you're all set.

7. What if I feel like giving up?

It takes courage to try anything, and when you imagine failure, it feels bad. If you give up, you may feel relieved. But that relief will last for only a few minutes. After that, you are likely to feel unhappy with yourself until you decide to pick up where you left off. Sticking with the process offers you the opportunity to free yourself from panic and all the limits it places on your life.

8. Should I link to a picture of the calming person, rather than just a memory?

I believe the best picture is the memory you have in your mind. A person does not look at a camera the same way they look at you in a moment of attunement or intimacy. Genuine calming signals are usually not produced when posing, although a candid photograph might capture them. If you want to try a photograph, notice what you feel when looking at it.

9. Does the linking need to be done in private?

Ordinarily, you do the exercise by linking a stressful situation to the memory of a calming person. But you can link the stressful situation to a calming person you are with. If you do link to an actual person, try the exercise also in private, to see which works best for you.

CHAPTER 21

Emotional Control
in Panic-Inducing Situations

I received the following message from a client:

> *I wanted to email you a little info for you to use in case you would like. I signed up for your program without much real hope that it would work. I was "that guy" who boarded a plane, sat down and before the door was closed, faked a phone call of some urgency as an excuse to deplane. They were very low points for me. I thought I would see if it was even possible for me to be comfortable flying. I'm thrilled and even shocked to say, your program worked, and worked completely.*

This chapter explores common situations that can induce panic. Many of them are situations in which there seems to be no way to escape. When the release of stress hormones alerts the amygdala that something is nonroutine, executive function needs to determine whether it is an opportunity, a threat, or a matter of no interest. When a situation offers no escape, executive function may not take the time to accurately assess the potential threat: it may shoot first and ask questions later.

We know MRI machines, for example, are safe. We know bridges, tunnels, and elevators are safe. Even so, they threaten emotional danger. Once inside, you seem to be stuck. If you demand to be let out of an MRI machine, of course, the technician will let you out. If you're riding an elevator, the door will open at your floor; even if the elevator gets stuck, you'll be rescued. But that takes time. When panic kicks in, your mobilization system demands immediate escape.

Panic in situations that are safe but offer no escape can be prevented in two ways: by inhibiting the release of stress hormones that cause feelings that can be mistaken for danger, and by establishing links to a person whose face, voice, and touch activate the calming parasympathetic nervous system. Prevention requires preparation. The following exercises prepare you, over several days, to face such situations without panic.

When doing a linking exercise, we need to make it as stress-free as possible. We don't try to link the whole situation to a calming influence. Rather, we break the potentially stressful situation down into as many pieces as possible and then link each piece to a calming influence, one piece at a time. Some situations need to be broken down into more pieces than others.

Preparing for an MRI

Day 1

Link the sequence of events that will take place to a memory that causes oxytocin production. Imagine watching a cartoon character go through this sequence.

- Imagine the cartoon character at home.
- The character leaves home.
- The character is in a car, driving to the imaging facility.
- The character checks in at the imaging facility.
- A technician invites the character to leave the waiting room.
- The character follows the technician into the MRI area.
- The cartoon character changes into an exam gown.
- The character removes metal objects like jewelry and watches.
- The technician invites the character to recline on the MRI bed.
- The character's head is placed on the headrest.
- The technician adjusts the height of the bed.
- The character waits for things to begin.
- The bed begins to move slowly.
- The character hears loud buzzing, chirping, and jackhammering sounds.
- The bed moves the character slowly into the tunnel.
- The character's head enters the tunnel.
- The bed moves the character's body into the tunnel.

- The bed moves the character through the tunnel.
- The character's face is out of the tunnel.
- The character is completely out of the tunnel.
- The technician invites the character to get up from the bed.
- The cartoon character changes back into regular clothing.
- The cartoon character leaves the facility.
- The character drives home.
- The character is back home.

Day 2

Link the sequence of events to a memory that produces vagal braking.

Day 3

Repeat day 1.

Day 4

Repeat day 2.

Day 5

Make a list of everything you can think of that could go wrong. Some common concerns are these:

- What if I can't breathe?
- What if I have a heart attack?
- What if I can't get help?

- What if the panic doesn't go away?
- What if I lose control?
- What if I go crazy?
- What if they find something wrong?
- What if I find out I'm going to die?

Using your imagination, produce a "what if" thought cartoon. Put a "what if" thought in the mind of a cartoon character. Place the thought in a balloon over the cartoon character's head. Link the cartoon to a memory that stimulates oxytocin production. Repeat until every "what if" thought has been linked to oxytocin production.

Day 6

Link each "what if" thought cartoon to a memory that stimulates vagal braking. Continue until every "what if" thought has been linked to vagal braking.

Day 7

Link each "what if" thought cartoon to a memory that causes oxytocin production.

Day 8

Once again, link each "what if" thought cartoon to a memory that stimulates vagal braking.

Day 9

Repeat day 1.

Day 10

Repeat day 2.

You have finished the preparation for your MRI.

Preparing for a Visit to a High Place

Being afraid of high places, even when we know rationally that we are in no danger of falling, is very common. This fear is partly rooted in the way our vision system processes information. Our eyes are spaced slightly apart, and as a result, each eye sends a slightly different image to the visual processing area of the brain. The difference between the two images is what enables us to perceive depth and distance and maintain our balance. When we look at an object or scene more than thirty feet away, this difference becomes too small for us to sense it. In the view from a high place, such as the top of a building, everything is more than thirty feet away. Nevertheless, our eyes and brain keep searching for an object to fix on that will help us maintain our balance. Our vision zooming in and out may throw our balance off and even cause vertigo. When our sense of balance is impaired in a high place, a fear of falling is understandable.

In a high place, immediate escape is available by jumping. Since jumping is likely to be fatal, if the idea comes to mind, it is shocking. That shock — plus the thought that the urge to escape might become overwhelming and cause you to lose control and jump — can trigger panic in high places.

A high place can also be overwhelming because there is too much to take in all at once. Years ago, I went to Venice with a friend. We visited Saint Mark's Basilica, which has a high balcony that offers a magnificent view of the huge Saint Mark's Square and all of Venice and the harbor in the distance. I took her out there, and suddenly she said, "Get me out of here!" My first thought was, "What? We *are* out."

She continued yelling, "Get me out of here, get me out of here!" Not knowing what else to do, I took her back inside.

She said, "You knew better than to do that."

I asked, "What are you talking about?"

"It's too much!" she shouted. To me, it was marvelous looking out and seeing all of Venice. I looked down at a cafe, at the pigeons, at people walking, at the tower, at rooftops, at the harbor.

The difference between us was that I took in those objects one by one. My friend was overwhelmed because she tried to take them in all at once. It is executive function's job to do a quick take of the situation, decide what is most important, deal with that, and then attend to the next most important thing, and so forth, like the triage process in an emergency room. An overwhelmed emergency room, full of patients calling for immediate attention, doesn't function well. Nor does executive function when it is overwhelmed with too many things to process at once.

We can protect executive function from the feeling of overwhelm by imagining the feeling in the mind of a cartoon character and linking it to the face, voice, and touch of a person whose calming presence stimulates vagal braking. We can also imagine focusing on only one thing in our field of view at a time, with the support of a calming friend.

Another problem with being up high is lack of immediate escape (short of jumping). It takes time to get back down on the ground. When my friend was overwhelmed, she demanded that I get her "out of here." She didn't believe she could get out on her own. When her executive function was overwhelmed, she could not even think clearly enough to turn around and go back through the doorway she had just passed through. In a state of panic, we need an immediately visible escape route. If the exit is not in view — even if it is easily accessible — the overwhelmed person believes no exit is possible and may feel helplessly trapped. Sometimes, even when the exit is visible, the person is frozen to the spot because their immobilization system is activated. They see the door or the stairs but cannot use them.

If you are afraid of heights, I think you ought to cut yourself some slack about it. It is completely normal to feel anxious when your balance mechanism is impaired. But if you know you're going to have to face such a situation, this exercise can help you manage feelings of anxiety and overwhelm.

Day 1

Link the following sequence of events to a memory that causes oxytocin production.

- Imagine a cartoon character thinking about going up to a high place.
- Imagine the character ascending to a high place.
- Imagine the character in a high place.
- The character is looking out at the scene.
- The character notices things look strangely flat.
- The character notices that things in view seem odd, a bit unreal.

- Imagine the character descending from the high place.
- Imagine the character back on the ground.
- Imagine the character back at home.

Day 2

Link the sequence of events above to a memory that causes vagal braking.

Day 3

Link the more detailed steps below to a memory that produces oxytocin.

- Imagine a cartoon character thinking about going up to a high place.
- Imagine the character ascending to the high place.
- Imagine the character remembering to focus on only one thing at a time.
- Imagine the character looking out at the scene.
- Imagine the character looking out at the scene and selecting one thing to focus on.
- Imagine the character looking out at the scene and selecting another thing to focus on.
- Imagine the character looking out at the scene and selecting yet another thing to focus on.
- Imagine the character descending from the high place.
- Imagine the character back on the ground.
- Imagine the character back at home.

Day 4

Link the steps for day 3 to a memory that causes vagal braking.

Day 5

Link the following steps to a memory that produces oxytocin.

- Imagine a cartoon character thinking about going to a high place.
- Imagine the character ascending to a high place while making an internal map of the pathway to reach it.
- Imagine the cartoon character looking out at the vista and at the same time remaining aware of how to reach the exit.
- Imagine the cartoon character selecting something to focus on while remaining aware of how to reach the exit.
- Imagine the cartoon character selecting another thing to focus on while remaining aware of how to reach the exit.
- Imagine the cartoon character selecting yet another thing to focus on while remaining aware of how to reach the exit.
- Imagine the character returning to the exit by using the remembered path.
- Imagine the character descending from a high place by using the remembered path.
- Imagine the character back on the ground, having used the path held continuously in mind during the excursion.
- Imagine the character back at home, pleased to have maintained a continuous plan during the excursion.

Day 6

Link the steps for day 5 to a memory that causes vagal braking.

Day 7

List everything you can imagine going wrong during a visit to a high place. Some common concerns are these:

- What if I can't breathe?
- What if I have a heart attack?
- What if I can't get help?
- What if the panic doesn't go away?
- What if I lose control?
- What if I go crazy?
- What if I lose my balance and fall?

Add any additional thoughts you might have to this list. Using your imagination, produce a "what if" thought cartoon. Put a "what if" thought in the mind of a cartoon character. Place the thought in a balloon over the cartoon character's head. Link the cartoon to a memory that stimulates oxytocin production. Repeat until every "what if" thought has been linked to oxytocin production.

Day 8

Link each "what if" thought cartoon to a memory that stimulates vagal braking. Continue until every "what if" thought has been linked to vagal braking.

Day 9

Review the entire exercise by linking each item in all the lists to a memory that causes vagal braking.

Day 10

Review the entire exercise by linking each item in all the lists to a memory that produces oxytocin.

You have finished your preparation for your visit to a high place.

Preparing for Passage through a Tunnel

Many people fear tunnels because of the lack of an immediate escape. Even without delays, it takes time to travel through a tunnel. A person may fear panicking and having to endure the panic until they reach the tunnel exit. They may fear that unendurable panic will cause a heart attack. These fears may be compounded by the imagination of being stuck in the tunnel or of the tunnel collapsing.

The two fundamental elements of panic are present: believing that the situation is life-threatening and believing that it cannot be escaped. Stress hormones are released that disable reflective function, making the person unable to separate imagination from reality. Imagination takes over. The person experiences being trapped as powerfully as if it were really happening.

The solution is to keep reflective function working so that imagination is recognized as such and cannot overpower reality. To do this, we need to inhibit the release of stress hormones that disable reflective function by producing oxytocin, and to override the effect of any stress hormones released by stimulating vagal braking.

Day 1

Link the following sequence of events you will encounter to a memory that causes oxytocin production.

- Imagine a cartoon character thinking about going through a tunnel.
- Imagine the character getting in a car.
- Imagine the character heading toward a tunnel.
- Imagine the character seeing the tunnel in the distance.
- Imagine the character approaching the tunnel entrance.
- Imagine the character entering the tunnel.
- Imagine the character one-fourth of the way through the tunnel.
- Imagine the character halfway through the tunnel.
- Imagine the character three-quarters of the way through the tunnel.
- Imagine the character seeing light at the end of the tunnel.
- Imagine the character seeing the tunnel exit clearly.
- Imagine the character leaving the tunnel.
- Imagine the character well past the tunnel.
- Imagine the character arriving at the destination.

Day 2

Link the sequence of events above to a memory that causes vagal braking.

Day 3

Repeat the day 1 exercise to reinforce the links that cause oxytocin production.

Day 4

Repeat the day 2 exercise to reinforce the links that cause vagal braking.

Day 5

Make a list of everything you can think of that might go wrong. Some common concerns are these:

- What if I can't breathe?
- What if I have a heart attack?
- What if I can't get help?
- What if the panic doesn't go away?
- What if I lose control?
- What if I go crazy?
- What if I get stuck in traffic?
- What if there's an accident and the tunnel is completely blocked?
- What if the tunnel collapses?
- What if I'm going to die?

Add any additional concerns you may have to the list. Using your imagination, produce a "what if" thought cartoon. Put a "what if" thought in the mind of a cartoon character. Place the thought in a balloon over the cartoon character's head. Link the cartoon to a memory that stimulates oxytocin production. Repeat until every "what if" thought has been linked to oxytocin production.

Day 6

Link each "what if" thought cartoon to a memory that stimulates vagal braking. Continue until every "what if" thought has been linked to vagal braking.

Day 7

Repeat the day 5 exercise to reinforce the links that cause oxytocin production.

Day 8

Repeat the day 6 exercise to reinforce the links that stimulate vagal braking.

Day 9

Repeat the day 1 exercise to reinforce links to a memory that causes oxytocin production.

Day 10

Repeat the day 2 exercise to reinforce links to a memory that stimulates vagal braking.

You have completed your preparation.

Preparing to Cross a Bridge

Automobile bridges, elevated walkways, and rope or cable footbridges can induce panic because they combine being high up with having no way to escape. There may also be fear that the bridge could collapse, plunging the person into an abyss or water under the bridge. The following exercises can help alleviate these fears.

Day 1

Link the following sequence of events you will encounter to a memory that causes oxytocin production.

- Imagine a cartoon character thinking about crossing a bridge.
- Imagine the character heading toward the bridge.
- Imagine the character seeing the bridge in the distance.
- Imagine the character approaching the bridge.
- Imagine the character going onto the bridge.
- Imagine the character one-fourth of the way across the bridge.
- Imagine the character halfway across the bridge.
- Imagine the character three-quarters of the way across the bridge.
- Imagine the character seeing the end of the bridge.
- Imagine the character leaving the bridge.
- Imagine the character well past the bridge.
- Imagine the character arriving at the destination.

Day 2

The following day, link the same sequence of events to a memory that causes vagal braking.

Day 3

Repeat linking to a memory that produces oxytocin.

Day 4

Repeat linking to a memory that causes vagal braking.

Day 5

Make a list of everything you can think of that might go wrong. Put each in the mind of a cartoon character. Some common concerns are these:

- What if I can't breathe?
- What if I have a heart attack?
- What if I can't get help?
- What if the panic doesn't go away?
- What if I lose control?
- What if I go crazy?
- What if the bridge collapses?
- What if I'm going to die?

Add any additional "what if" thoughts you may have. Using your imagination, produce a "what if" thought cartoon. Put a "what if" thought in the mind of a cartoon character. Place the thought in a balloon over the cartoon character's head. Link the cartoon to a memory that stimulates oxytocin production. Repeat until every "what if" thought has been linked to oxytocin production.

Day 6

Link each "what if" thought cartoon to a memory that stimulates vagal braking. Continue until every "what if" thought has been linked to vagal braking.

Day 7

Repeat the day 5 exercise to reinforce the links that cause oxytocin production.

Day 8

Repeat the day 6 exercise to reinforce the links that stimulate vagal braking.

Day 9

Repeat the day 1 exercise to reinforce links to a memory that causes oxytocin production.

Day 10

Repeat the day 2 exercise to reinforce links to a memory that stimulates vagal braking.

You have completed your preparation.

CHAPTER 22

Controlling Anxiety

A former fear-of-flying client emailed the following:

> *What you taught me did wonders. I have no panic at all. It worked so well that I'm wondering if it can help me with my new job. For the first time I'm a supervisor. When someone asks a question and I don't know the answer, I get extremely anxious. I feel like I'm in over my head. My boss says I'm doing a good job. But, I feel the same when I'm talking to him. I've thought about quitting. But, I moved here to take this job, and I can't handle moving back.*

So far this book has focused on panic. Now let's look at anxiety. What are some of the differences between panic and anxiety? In panic, a person believes their life is threatened and that escape from the threat is impossible. With anxiety, the threat is not life-threatening. Escape is possible, but it has drawbacks: it may involve compromise or some kind of cost or loss. Fortunately, we can apply the same techniques we use for ending panic to ending anxiety.

When stressed by face-to-face interactions, my client felt an urge to escape. If he had been in a situation where escape was blocked, he would have experienced panic. Since escape was possible in this situation, he did not panic, but he was anxious that he would lose control, the urge to flee would overwhelm him, and he would cut and run. If he did, he would be fired, and his self-esteem would be damaged.

How could we make him comfortable at work? To establish a basis for collaboration, I told him about the system responsible for regulating our arousal — the autonomic nervous system, described in part 2 of this book — and explained how he could now install the alarm attenuation mechanisms that he did not develop in childhood.

In his previous job, my client worked with others at the same level. They frequently exchanged signals that kept things calm. In his new job, he received no calming signals from the employees he supervised. When in control, he was calm. But when he could not immediately answer a question, he felt he was not in control of the situation. As he said, "I feel like I'm in over my head." Stress hormones kicked in. With no built-in program to activate vagal braking, the urge to escape threatened to overwhelm him.

Dealing with this situation was simple. All we needed to do was build in a psychologically active presence that could activate his parasympathetic nervous system when he was face to face with people who did not provide calming signals. To do that, we needed to find a person in his life whose presence calmed him. He quickly identified someone, an easygoing, nonjudgmental friend. I asked him if he had felt his guard let down when with this friend, an indication of maximum parasympathetic nervous system activation. He said he did. That made her an ideal person to link to his challenges at work.

Together, we started looking for ways to link the calming signals of her face, voice, and touch to his work situations. I asked him to remember being with her. I asked him to imagine that she was holding a photo of one of his employees next to her face. In a few seconds, a link was established between the calming face of his friend and the noncalming face of the employee. This link neutralized the employee's face as a threat. Then I asked him to imagine talking with his friend about the photo (to link the calming quality of her voice to the challenging situation). Then while talking, I asked him to imagine her giving him a reassuring touch.

For extra protection, we linked her face, voice, and touch to a cartoon of Homer Simpson being unable to answer an employee's question. We then linked the friend's qualities to an image of Homer worrying about being in over his head in a new job.

Next, we turned to his boss. We linked the friend's face, voice, and touch to the boss's face. Since my client was often afraid of what his boss would say, we took the linking a step further. Instead of imagining her holding a photo of the boss talking, I asked him to imagine she was holding a cell phone playing a video of his boss talking.

Another client emailed me as follows:

I need help with social anxiety and speaking in groups/ public. I use the techniques to control anxiety when flying. My hope is that the techniques will work for other forms of anxiety as well.

As you have seen, when we lack automatic alarm attenuation, we try to control things so that nothing alarming
happens to us. Although it often results from a lack of attuned caregiving in childhood, the need to control can be
an advantage in careers such as business or law. This was the
case for my client, who worked for a few years as an accoun-
tant. Being very bright, he quickly learned the workings of
the businesses he provided services for, and soon set up a
company of his own.

Because he was good at controlling things, his business
prospered. He hired more and more employees, some of
whom were older, highly experienced businessmen. Even
though they were his employees, his shyness made interacting with them difficult. He had not explained this in his
email, but when negotiating a contract, he could maintain
eye contact only when he felt he was in a dominant position.
When less sure of himself, visual disengagement put him
into a weaker negotiating position.

Like my first client, he was uncomfortable in a business
setting because, in this role, the signals he received from the
people he interacted with did not calm him. Looking into
how he could feel comfortable, I found that he did have internal resources that could calm him. The problem was that
these resources were not active when he did business. To
down-regulate his anxiety in business situations, we linked
his internal resources to the business environment and to
the various challenges associated with it.

Could we prevent stress hormone release when he was
speaking in public? Of course. He had a dog. As we know,
we release oxytocin when we interact with dogs. In preparation for public speaking, I asked him to go to the room
ahead of time and project a mental image of his dog looking

at him onto various surfaces of the room. I wanted him to embed his dog's attentive face into those surfaces, so that as he glanced naturally around the room while giving his presentation, the embedded images of his dog would stimulate the release of oxytocin.

If he began to feel anxious, could we activate vagal braking as he spoke? Of course. He only needed to bring to mind a person who activated his parasympathetic nervous system and project an image of that person's face onto those same surfaces and some items that would be in view as he spoke.

I've taught people to use this approach in other anxiety-provoking situations, including pilot training. Some trainee pilots are comfortable when their flight instructor is in the cockpit with them but experience anxiety when flying solo. They can regulate anxiety by linking an oxytocin-producing memory and a vagal-braking activating memory to each item on their standard preflight checklist and to every switch they touch in the cockpit.

For additional protection against intimidation during negotiations, we linked an imaginary cellphone video of the person my client would be meeting with to the face, voice, and touch of the person who stimulated his parasympathetic nervous system.

He asked also about regulating anxiety in situations he could not prepare for in advance, so we worked on establishing automatic alarm attenuation. For the next few days, instead of trying to avoid awareness of anxiety, he looked for it so that he could notice it at the lowest perceptible threshold. Then he immediately imagined that the calming person had just walked into the room. He visualized the person greeting him, coming over to him, and giving him a friendly or affectionate touch.

The techniques in this book can also be used to manage anxieties arising from personal relationships. Though relationships are sometimes stressful, humans still need them. We can't always count on a romantic partner, a spouse, a friend, or a family member to calm us; in fact, sometimes those relationships are sources of additional stress. The obvious answer to better relationships is to develop internal resources that will activate our parasympathetic nervous system when needed.

One way or another, alarm attenuation depends on others. The only question is whether the calming person is physically beside us or psychologically inside us.

Search your memory for a moment when the presence of another person caused your guard to let down. If you don't recall such a moment, call to mind a person you feel genuinely at ease with. Link that person's face, voice, and touch to each relational challenge in your life.

CHAPTER 23

Summary

A client who had been troubled by panic when flying emailed the following:

> *I know from experience how effective the SOAR approach is. I am reassured because SOAR gets to the root of why I feel the way I do and that enables me to assess all types of stressful situations that I can now manage by not letting the naturally occurring stress hormones overwhelm me.*

Reading this book can give you insight, but insight alone will most likely not stop panic. To stop panic, you will need to go back to chapter 21, and for the next ten days or so carry out the assigned tasks.

Training is key. Under extreme stress, we do not *rise* to the occasion; we *descend* to the level of our training. Through repetition, unconscious procedural memory is trained to regulate arousal automatically. Since it is located in the subcortex, it operates well even under stress.

Here, at the end of the book, I'm reminded of an email from a client who had struggled for years with panic. He and I did a few counseling sessions by phone. After studying the information that I've now put into book form, and practicing the exercises I gave him, he became panic free.

Usually at that point, clients are overjoyed. He was different: he was annoyed. He had consulted a number of experts and applied the advice they gave him. He said he had read every book on the subject. Looking back at his struggle, he said, "I gave it my all. And it didn't work. Why isn't *this* information out there, everywhere?"

Now it is.

Afterword for Therapists

BY STEPHEN W. PORGES, PhD

Panic and Anxiety: Maladaptive Manifestations of an Adaptive Neurobiological Defense Mechanism

In *Panic Free* Tom Bunn shares his insights in treating and regulating panic and severe anxiety. *Panic Free* provides a platform to expand his insights from treating flying-related fears to more general contexts. In his earlier book, *SOAR: The Breakthrough Treatment for Fear of Flying*, he used his experience as a pilot and therapist to discuss the power of easily identified flight-related fear-inducing triggers. Through decades of work with individuals who experienced an intolerable and debilitating fear of flying, Bunn developed a reliable model of treatment. In *Panic Free* he expands the application of his treatment model to deal with the anxiety and panic attacks that may occur in other situations and contexts.

Based on his experiences treating clients with fear of flying, Bunn has extracted principles to constrain the progressive trajectory of dysregulation that characterizes the transition from mild anxiety to a complete panic attack. In *Panic Free* he applies these principles as an effective strategy to enhance the self-regulation of bodily and emotional states that become disrupted during panic and extreme levels of anxiety. The resultant product is an accessible guide for the client with methods to constrain the progressive trajectory of dysregulation.

In developing his innovative therapeutic model, Bunn has drawn from his professional experiences and from contemporary neuroscience (e.g., Polyvagal Theory). These two domains enable him to understand the observable feelings and thoughts that accompany high levels of anxiety and panic through the lens of neuroscience. From decades of treating clients with "fear of flying," he creates a pathway of treatment. He accomplishes this through interdependent processes embedded in his treatment model that can be summarized as: (1) systematic deconstruction of the triggers that elicit subjective states of anxiety and panic, (2) witnessing and acknowledging the sequence of bodily feelings and reactions that the client experiences on the trajectory from mild anxiety to an intolerable panic attack, (3) providing the client with a neurobiologically informed explanation of the visceral, motoric, and mental states that the client experiences during transitions from calmness to anxiety and panic, (4) providing the client with neurobiologically informed exercises based on understanding the potency of changing the client's physiological state in dampening and constraining anxiety and panic, and (5) extracting neurobiologically informed principles to recover resilience that have worked with fear of flying. In *Panic Free* he applies these principles to other anxiety-eliciting experiences, such as driving through tunnels or over bridges, that for many clients are profound triggers capable of disrupting a calm emotional state and eliciting intolerable states of anxiety and panic.

Frequently, even in the clinical world, there is a misunderstanding of the mechanisms underlying anxiety and panic. Rather than interpreting anxiety and panic responses as the body's attempt to protect itself, there is often an implicit (and sometimes explicit) assumption that these disruptions in self-regulation have a voluntary or intentional component. The vulnerable individual, who has a low threshold to respond with intense anxiety and panic, is frequently chastised as having failed to voluntarily control their behavior. Having poor self-regulation often limits opportunities to create relationships and to participate fully in society. This lack of social success may lead to self-blame and poor self-esteem. In many situations, the individual with these features is subjected to additional criticisms leading to shame, rather than receiving the compassionate and compensatory support that might contribute to rehabilitation and resilience. We see examples of this in the mismatch between the needs of vulnerable individuals and the reactions of others in the community, including educators, medical professionals, and managers in the workplace.

A conceptualization of anxiety and panic as having a voluntary component is faulty, and this becomes obvious when perceived through the lens of Polyvagal Theory. Polyvagal Theory provides the neurophysiological basis to reinterpret anxiety and panic as "reflexive" adaptive self-protective reactions and *not* voluntary responses with the intent to disrupt. Thus, directives to voluntarily control anxiety as it is ramping up to a panic attack are doomed to fail. Attributing

intention to an individual experiencing high levels of anxiety and panic will make the experience worse by exacer-
bating the physiological reactions that support extreme and
intolerable anxiety and panic.

In *Panic Free* Bunn skillfully incorporates features of
Polyvagal Theory into a powerful treatment model for
anxiety and panic. First, he applies the theory to provide
a neurobiologically informed explanation of the mental and behavioral features that define intolerable anxiety
and panic. Polyvagal Theory identifies an autonomic state
driven by activation of the sympathetic nervous system that
supports mobilized defense. This is the physiological state
that supports the trajectory from mild anxiety to panic. It
is frequently associated with high states of arousal and provides the metabolic resources for fight and flight behaviors.

Second, he applies the polyvagal construct of neuroception as a mechanism through which cues in the environment
reflexively trigger shifts in physiological state. Neuroception
occurs without a conscious awareness of the specific triggers. However, as in the case of an individual experiencing
intolerable anxiety and panic, the visceral reactions are sufficiently potent to reach a level of conscious awareness and
become associated with context. This produces a sequence
that is initiated by our nervous system detecting the risk,
then our body responds to the risk, and finally we become
aware of the risk. Given this sequence, we may make mistakes in accurately identifying the triggers and their source.
At times we may create a faulty narrative that does not link
the visceral feelings with the effective trigger. Sometimes we
miss the actual trigger and attribute the cause of the disruption to another event or person.

Third, Bunn applies an understanding of the hierarchy

of the neural circuits regulating autonomic function described in the theory. This hierarchy parallels the evolution of neural regulation of the autonomic nervous system in vertebrates. Phylogenetically the sequence starts with an immobilization system that slows metabolic activity through an ancient vagal pathway that initially appears in primitive vertebrates and is still functional in humans and other mammals. When this ancient system is recruited in defense, it is associated with a behavioral shutdown (e.g., death feigning) and potentially a numbness of the body leading to dissociation. The phylogenetic sequence is followed by the aforementioned sympathetic nervous system that provides the metabolic resource for fight and flight behaviors. Finally, as mammals evolved, the neural regulation of the autonomic nervous system took on another attribute that enabled conspecifics to communicate cues of safety and trust through an integrated social engagement system. This system connected the nerves regulating the muscles of the face and head with a vagal pathway to the heart, which has the capacity to down-regulate sympathetic states of defense. Thus, a recruitment of the social engagement system, via facial expression and intonation of voice, has the capacity to down-regulate defenses and calm the autonomic nervous system sufficiently to experience immobilization without fear, a state that enables feelings of safety, trust, and intimacy. Underlying these profound changes in emotional and behavioral state are two interrelated mechanisms: (1) a neural pathway through a uniquely mammalian myelinated vagal pathway that provides an efficient "vagal brake" to slow cardiac output and calm behavior, and (2) a neurochemical pathway through which oxytocin fosters immobilization without fear (e.g., intimacy) that is experienced as feelings of safety, trust, and love.

An additional relevant construct related to the phylogenetic hierarchy of autonomic regulation is dissolution. Dissolution was introduced by the philosopher Herbert Spencer (1820–1903) to describe evolution in reverse. It was adapted by John Hughlings Jackson (1835–1911) to describe how brain damage and brain disease function similarly to a process of "de-evolution" in which evolutionarily older circuits become disinhibited. Polyvagal Theory adapts dissolution to explain the phylogenetically ordered hierarchy in which the autonomic nervous system responds with progressively evolutionarily older circuits. Neuroception is the process that triggers the change in physiological state along this hierarchy and, thus, can either elicit or constrain anxiety. To elicit anxiety, neuroception would trigger a "dissolution" from a physiological state that supports feelings of safety (i.e., social engagement system with a functional vagal brake to a physiological state that supports anxiety and panic — i.e., the sympathetic nervous system).

Fourth, Bunn leverages the power of neuroception in calming disruptive states by recruiting potent memories of select moments of safety, love, intimacy, and benevolent care. These memories function, as with the presence of a loving supportive person, as a powerful top-down process capable of activating the social engagement system and constraining defenses. It is this simple, yet brilliant, technique that provides the "magic" to the treatment model. When the client is encouraged to reexperience these idealized moments, the nervous system is functionally processing (via neuroception) the visualized positive cues of vocal intonation, facial expression, inviting gesture, and gentle touch.

The reexperiencing of memories evokes a powerful shift in neural regulation of physiological state via enhanced functioning of the vagal brake and the release of oxytocin.

Panic Free provides an objective, neurophysiologically informed treatment model. As outlined above, as long as our autonomic nervous system is not recruited for defense, anxiety and panic are not problems. However, life is not without challenges that trigger defensive states. In select contexts, defensive states may breed feelings of anxiety that may lead to panic. Fortunately, our nervous system has circuits that have the capacity to constrain our need to fight or flee. Humans, similar to other mammals, have an integrated social engagement system that evolved to signal and detect cues of safety. Detection of these cues through neuroception enables individuals to feel safe in each other's arms. *Panic Free* emphasizes that the moments when we are safe and intimate with others provide a resource that can be recruited through the reenactment of memories to constrain anxiety and to shift the individual into a calm state. *Panic Free* informs us that by building our resilience through the reenactments of memories, we are never alone.

Neuroscientist **Stephen W. Porges, PhD,** *a recipient of the National Institute of Mental Health Research Scientist Development Award, is a professor of psychiatry at the University of North Carolina. He formerly directed the Brain-Body Center at the University of Illinois at Chicago and was president of the Society for Psychophysiological Research and of the Federation of Behavioral, Psychological and Cognitive Sciences. His Polyvagal Theory provides insight into human relatedness.*

APPENDIX

Supporting Research

My book *SOAR: The Breakthrough Treatment for Fear of Flying*, published in 2013, devoted only part of one chapter to panic. Even so, a number of readers found that it contained everything they needed to know to control panic. Several who posted online reviews of the book said they experienced panic when flying (some even experienced it when only thinking of flying) prior to reading the book and no panic afterward.

To get a better idea of how effective the SOAR techniques are for overcoming panic, I asked a randomly selected group of graduates of the SOAR Guaranteed Fear of Flying Program whether they experienced panic on the ground or in the air before and after taking the course. The "guaranteed" course includes two hours of counseling and offers a full refund if the client is unsatisfied with the improvement when flying. Enrollees in the guaranteed course are our toughest clients. Many say they have tried every method to combat fear of flying, without success, and they want a guarantee because they don't expect the course to work. All eleven graduates who responded to the questionnaire reported that prior to taking the course, they experienced panic when flying, and six reported experiencing panic on the ground as well. After the course, nine of the eleven no longer experienced panic in the air.

Though the course is aimed at eliminating panic in the air, it also helped clients to reduce panic on the ground. Five of the six who had previously had panic attacks on the ground became panic free there, too.

How does this compare with the most commonly used therapy for panic, cognitive behavioral therapy (CBT)? In a 2005 study of 105 patients who received CBT and anti-anxiety medication, 29 percent reported no panic attacks after 12 months. Another study, published in 2000, surveyed 312 patients with panic disorder. It found that after six months, 39.5 percent of the participants responded to CBT. But 13 percent had responded to placebo treatment. Thus the CBT response rate was only 26.5 percent higher than the placebo treatment response rate. ("Response" refers to improvement, not complete freedom from panic.)

The study of SOAR Guaranteed Program clients was followed by a larger study of a much shorter SOAR fear-of-flying course. Of the eighty-nine who reported panic when flying prior to the course, sixty (about 67 percent) reported no panic, and sixteen reported less panic after the course. Sixty-nine people reported panic on the ground prior to the course. After the course, forty reported no panic, and nine reported less panic.

Both of these SOAR courses focused exclusively on dealing with panic when flying. This book, because it focuses on managing panic on the ground, should produce a cure rate much closer to 100 percent.

Acknowledgments

None of the answers this book provides would have been possible without the courage and tenacity of clients who were willing to grapple with their panic until, together, we found a solution. I am grateful to the clients who generously contributed to this book by sharing their struggles with the problem.

Much of the success we have achieved is based on studies with James F. Masterson, Ralph Klein, Judith Pearson, and Allan Schore. Mentalization concepts developed by Peter Fonagy and associates are essential to understanding the cause of panic. Polyvagal Theory, developed by Stephen W. Porges, is essential to understanding how panic can be cured.

My mentors Cynthia P. Deutsch, Elaine Rapp, and Glen Boles encouraged me to undertake the professional studies that led to a solution to panic — and thus to this book.

Janet Rosen provided invaluable editing advice. Time and again, Georgia Hughes, Erika Büky, and Kristen Cashman — seemingly effortlessly — came out with text that perfectly communicated what I had struggled with. The book is also based on long discussions with my wife, Marie, whose insights into anxiety and panic were invaluable.

Notes

Chapter 1: A Future Free of Panic and Claustrophobia

p. 7   *She came up with a technique she called "thought stopping"*: Jerilyn Ross, *Triumph Over Fear* (New York: Bantam Books, 1995), 94.

p. 8   *Research by Sue Carter, Kerstin Uvnäs Moberg, and others*: C. Sue Carter, Jessie R. Williams, Diane M. Witt, and Thomas R. Insel, "Oxytocin and Social Bonding," *Annals of the New York Academy of Sciences* 652, no. 1 (1992): 204–11; Kerstin Uvnäs Moberg, "Antistress Pattern Induced by Oxytocin," *News in Physiological Sciences* 27 (1998): 22–26; Inga Neumann, Simone Krömer, Nicola Toschi, and Karl Ebner, "Brain Oxytocin Inhibits the (Re)Activity of the Hypothalamo-Pituitary-Adrenal Axis in Male Rats: Involvement of Hypothalamic and Limbic Brain Regions," *Regulatory Peptides* 96 (2000): 31–38.

Chapter 3: Carole's Holland Tunnel Challenge

p. 20   *Stephen Porges refers to this process as* vagal braking: Stephen W. Porges, "The Polyvagal Perspective," *Biological Psychology* 74, no. 2 (2007): 121–22.

Chapter 5: How Arousal Regulation Works

p. 29   *"the most important aspect of the earliest mother-infant relationship"*: Heinz Kohut, *The Analysis of the Self: A Systematic Approach to Psychoanalytic Treatment of Narcissistic Personality Disorders* (Chicago: University of Chicago Press, 2009), 64.

p. 30   *This primitive system, which Porges calls the* mobilization system: Stephen W. Porges, *The Polyvagal Theory: Neurophysiological*

Foundations of Emotions, Attachment, Communication, and Self-Regulation (New York: W. W. Norton, 2011), 160.

p. 32   *This system, which Porges calls the* social engagement system: Stephen W. Porges, "The Polyvagal Theory: Phylogenetic Substrates of a Social Nervous System," *International Journal of Psychophysiology* 42, no. 2 (2001): 124.

p. 32   *Porges refers to this overriding by the vagus nerve as* vagal braking: Porges, "The Polyvagal Theory," 129–30.

p. 32   *"Nobody then anticipated* how *dependent the infant's* brain *was"*: James S. Grotstein, foreword to *Affect Regulation and the Origin of the Self: The Neurobiology of Emotional Development* by Allan N. Schore (Hillsdale, NJ: Lawrence Erlbaum Associates, 1994), xxiv.

p. 32   *"unconditional positive regard"*: Carl Rogers, "The Necessary and Sufficient Conditions of Therapeutic Personality Change," *Journal of Consulting Psychology* 21, no. 2 (1957): 96.

p. 32   *Harry Harlow showed that baby monkeys preferred soft dolls*: Stephen J. Suomi and Helen A. Leroy, "In Memoriam: Harry F. Harlow (1905–1981)," *American Journal of Primatology* 2 (1982), 319–42.

p. 33   *John Bowlby showed that infants need relationship*: John Bowlby, *A Secure Base: Parent-Child Attachment and Healthy Human Development* (New York: Basic Books, 1988), 119–36.

p. 33   *Every child is "constitutionally primed"*: Anthony W. Bateman and Peter Fonagy, *Mentalization-Based Treatment for Borderline Personality Disorder: A Practical Guide* (Oxford, UK: Oxford University Press, 2006), 15.

p. 35   *Research at the University of Arizona*: Kyle J. Bourassa, John M. Ruiz, David A. Sbarra, "The Impact of Physical Proximity and Attachment Working Models on Cardiovascular Reactivity: Comparing Mental Activation and Romantic Partner Presence," *Psychophysiology* (January 2019), https://onlinelibrary.wiley.com/doi/abs/10.1111/psyp.13324.

p. 36   *"It appears that thinking about your partner"*: Kyle J. Bourassa, quoted in "Stressed? Having a Partner Present — Even in Your Mind — May Keep Blood Pressure Down," *ScienceDaily*,

January 22,2019, www.sciencedaily.com/releases/2019/01
/190122153854.htm.

Chapter 8: Accepting Arousal as Normal

p. 51   *"We as a society think of spanking and physical abuse as distinct behaviors"*: Elizabeth T. Gershoff and Andrew Grogan-Kaylor, "Spanking and Child Outcomes: Old Controversies and New Meta-analyses," *Journal of Family Psychology* 30, no. 4 (June 2016): 453–69.

p. 52   *The child, and later the adult, is afraid*: Beatrice Beebe, Frank Lachmann, Sara Markese, Karen Buck, Lorraine Bahrick, and Henian Chen, "On the Origins of Disorganized Attachment and Internal Working Models," *Psychoanalytic Dialogues* 22 (2012): 361.

p. 52   *"Interactive experiences enable the child"*: Daniel J. Siegel, *The Developing Mind* (New York: Guilford Press, 1999), 247.

p. 53   *"Feeling felt"*: Siegel, *The Developing Mind*, 272.

p. 53   *It causes a child to feel abandoned and alone*: Beebe et al., "On the Origins of Disorganized Attachment."

p. 54   *"This inaccessible caregiver reacts to her infant's expressions of emotions"*: Allan N. Schore, *The Science of the Art of Psychotherapy* (New York: W. W. Norton, 2011), 124.

Chapter 9: How Feelings of Security and Insecurity Develop

p. 57   *"learn to trust both what they feel and how they understand the world"*: Bessel van der Kolk, "Developmental Trauma Disorder: Towards a Rational Diagnosis for Children with Complex Trauma Histories," *Psychiatric Annals* (2005): 403.

p. 57   *"if the distress is overwhelming"*: van der Kolk, "Developmental Trauma Disorder," 404.

p.59   *"interactions with people who teach the child"*: Julian D. Ford, *Treating Complex Traumatic Stress Disorders* (New York: Guilford Press, 2014), 34.

p. 59   *"lasting changes in the personality and the self occur"*: Ford, *Treating Complex Traumatic Stress Disorders*, 34.

p. 59 *"entrenched expectations of danger"*: Ford, *Treating Complex Traumatic Stress Disorders*, 34.

p. 60 *This phrase encapsulates the neurological theory presented by Donald Hebb*: Donald O. Hebb, *The Organization of Behavior* (New York: Wiley & Sons, 1949).

p. 62 *"Thus, not only is the onset of sympathetically driven fear-alarm states"*: Allan N. Schore, "The Effects of Early Relational Trauma on Right Brain Development, Affect Regulation, and Infant Mental Health," *Infant Mental Health Journal* 22 (2001): 201–69.

p. 64 *breathing exercises do not relieve panic*: Norman B. Schmidt, Kelly Woolaway-Bickel, Jack Trakowski, Helen Santiago, Julie Storey, Margaret Koselka, and Jeff Cook, "Dismantling Cognitive-Behavioral Treatment for Panic Disorder: Questioning the Utility of Breathing Retraining," *Journal of Consulting and Clinical Psychology* 68, no. 3 (2000): 417–24; Corine de Ruiter, Hanneke Rijken, Bert Garssen, and Floor Kraaimaat, "Breathing Retraining, Exposure and a Combination of Both, in the Treatment of Panic Disorder with Agoraphobia," *Behaviour Research and Therapy* 27, no. 6 (1989): 647–55; Simon Kim, Frances Palin, Page Anderson, Shannan Edwards, and Gretchen Lindner, "Use of Skills Learned in CBT for Fear of Flying: Managing Flying Anxiety after September 11th," *Journal of Anxiety Disorders* 22, no. 2 (2008): 301–9.

Chapter 10: Arousal Regulation Systems

p. 67 *regulation of arousal is first attempted by the most advanced system*: Stephen W. Porges and Deb A. Dana, eds., *Clinical Applications of the Polyvagal Theory: The Emergence of Polyvagal-Informed Therapies* (New York: W. W. Norton, 2018), 58.

p. 68 *Porges points out that, though primitive, the immobilization system*: Stephen W. Porges, *The Polyvagal Theory: Neurophysiological Foundations of Emotions, Attachment, Communication, and Self-Regulation* (New York: W. W. Norton, 2011), 159–60.

p. 71 *"internalized representations of relationships"*: Allan N. Schore,

Affect Regulation and the Repair of the Self (New York: W. W. Norton, 2003), 199.

p. 71 *Healthy regulation of arousal*: Schore, *Affect Regulation and the Repair of the Self*, 219, 257–58.

p. 73 *"What studies of resilience show is"*: Daniel J. Siegel, "Trauma, Brain & Relationship: Helping Children Heal," video (Palmyra, VA: Post Institute for Family Centered Therapy, March 12, 2013), https://youtu.be/jYyEEMlMMbo.

Chapter 11: The Arousal Regulation Hierarchy

p. 75 *According to Stephen Porges, down-regulation*: Stephen W. Porges, "The Polyvagal Theory: Phylogenetic Substrates of a Social Nervous System," *International Journal of Psychophysiology* 42, no. 2 (2001): 132.

Chapter 13: How Panic Is Triggered

p. 88 *Allan Schore has said that after a baby cries it out*: Allan N. Schore, *The Science of the Art of Psychotherapy* (New York: W. W. Norton, 2011), 439–40, and personal communication.

Chapter 15: Alarm Attenuation

p. 110 *"The child's first relationship"*: Allan N. Schore, *Affect Regulation and the Origin of the Self: The Neurobiology of Emotional Development* (Hillsdale, NJ: Lawrence Erlbaum Associates, 1994), 3.

p. 111 *"If I was a little baby, and I feel anxious"*: Peter Fonagy, "Peter Fonagy, Anna Freud Centre Chief Executive: What Is Mentalization? Interview," video (London: Anna Freud National Centre for Children and Families, March 11, 2015), https://www.youtube.com/watch?v=OHw2QumRPrQ.

p. 118 *Fonagy terms this state of mind* psychic equivalence: Peter Fonagy, György Gergely, Elliot Jurist, and Mary Target, *Affect Regulation, Mentalization, and the Development of the Self* (2002; reprint, New York: Other Press, 2004), 254–61.

Chapter 16: Establishing Automatic Alarm Attenuation

p. 123 *As Stephen Porges explains*: Stephen W. Porges and Deb A. Dana, eds., *Clinical Applications of the Polyvagal Theory: The Emergence of Polyvagal-Informed Therapies* (New York: W. W. Norton, 2018), 57–58.

Chapter 18: Strengthening Executive Function and Reflective Function

p. 138 *"hard-won developmental acquisition"*: Peter Fonagy, György Gergely, Elliot Jurist, and Mary Target, *Affect Regulation, Mentalization, and the Development of the Self* (2002; reprint, New York: Other Press, 2004), 254–61.

p. 140 *Freud proposed a distinction*: Sigmund Freud, *Totem and Taboo* (New York: W. W. Norton, 1990), 197–98.

p. 141 *"What characterizes neurotics is"*: Freud, *Totem and Taboo*, 198.

p. 141 *"Men would say of him that up he went"*: Plato, *The Republic: The Complete and Unabridged Jowett Translation* (New York: Penguin Random House, 1991), 257.

p. 141 *Freud regarded a preference for psychic reality as neurosis*: Freud, *Totem and Taboo*, 198.

p. 142 *"They experience ordinary negative self-evaluations"*: Anthony W. Bateman and Peter Fonagy, *Mentalization-Based Treatment for Borderline Personality Disorder: A Practical Guide* (Oxford, UK: Oxford University Press, 2006), 9.

p. 146 *people who maintain body awareness are better able to adapt*: Lori Haase, Jennifer Stewart, Brittany Youssef, April May, Sara Isakovic, Alan Simmons, Douglas Johnson, Eric Potterat, and Martin Paulus, "When the Brain Does Not Adequately Feel the Body: Links between Low Resilience and Interoception," *Biological Psychology* 113 (January 2016): 37–45.

Afterword for Therapists

p. 189 *this becomes obvious when perceived through the lens of Polyvagal Theory*: Stephen W. Porges, "The Polyvagal Perspective,"

Biological Psychology 74, no. 2 (2007): 116–43; Stephen W. Porges, *The Polyvagal Theory: Neurophysiological Foundations of Emotions, Attachment, Communication, and Self-Regulation* (New York: W.W. Norton, 2011); and Stephen W. Porges, *The Pocket Guide to the Polyvagal Theory: The Transformative Power of Feeling Safe* (New York: W.W. Norton, 2017).

p. 191   *a neural pathway through a uniquely mammalian myelinated vagal pathway*: Stephen W. Porges, Jane A. Doussard Roosevelt, A. Lourdes Portales, and Stanley I. Greenspan, "Infant Regulation of the Vagal 'Brake' Predicts Child Behavior Problems: A Psychobiological Model of Social Behavior," *Developmental Psychobiology* 29, no. 8 (1996): 697–712; Stephen W. Porges, "The Polyvagal Theory: Phylogenetic Substrates of a Social Nervous System," *International Journal of Psychophysiology* 42, no. 2 (2001): 123–46.

p. 191   *a neurochemical pathway through which oxytocin fosters immobilization*: C. Sue Carter, "The Oxytocin–Vasopressin Pathway in the Context of Love and Fear," *Frontiers in Endocrinology* 8 (2017): 356; C. Sue Carter and Stephen W. Porges, "The Biochemistry of Love: An Oxytocin Hypothesis (Science and Society Series on Sex and Science)," *EMBO Reports* 14, no. 1 (2013): 12–16.

p. 192   *It was adapted by John Hughlings Jackson*: J. Hughlings Jackson, "The Croonian Lectures on Evolution and Dissolution of the Nervous System," *British Medical Journal* 1, no. 1215 (April 12, 1884): 703–7.

Appendix: Supporting Research

p. 196   *In a 2005 study of 105 patients who received CBT*: Peter P. Roy-Byrne, Michelle G. Craske, Murray B. Stein, Greer Sullivan, Alexander Bystritsky, Wayne Katon, Daniela Golinelli, and Cathy D. Sherbourne, "A Randomized Effectiveness Trial of Cognitive Behavioral Therapy and Medication for Primary Care Panic Disorder," *Archives of General Psychiatry* 62, no. 3 (2005): 290–98, http://archpsyc.jamanetwork.com/article.aspx?article id=208417.

p. 196   *Another study, published in 2000*: David H. Barlow, Jack M. Gorman, M. Katherine Shear, and Scott W. Woods, "Cognitive-Behavioral Therapy, Imipramine, or Their Combination for Panic Disorder," *Journal of the American Medical Association* 283, no. 19 (2000): 2529–36.

Index

agoraphobia, 97

alarm, 58–59

alarm attenuation: author's experience, 113–16; automatic, 120, 123, 127, 153, 182, 183; child-caregiver relationship and, 110–11, 182; children and, 125; evolution of, 125; importance of, 111–13, 123; parasympathetic nervous system and, 123–25; reflective function and, 116–22, 149; relationship and, 184; role models and, 113–16; stress hormone effects overridden by, 113; during Ten-Day Plan, 156

alarm attenuation, establishment of, 180; age and, 131–32; Alarm Attenuation Exercise for, 129–31; arousal regulation systems and, 121–22; with calming person, 123–26; manual backup plan, 133–35; Three-Button Exercise for, 126–29, 156

Alarm Attenuation Exercise, 129–31

alarms, false, 114–15

alcoholism, 89, 144

ambiguity, 149

amygdala: arousal and, 58; change as activator of, 19–20, 113, 129, 161–62; claustrophobia and, 34; imaginary threats and, 71; imagination vs. perception and, 148; mobilization system and, 69; reptilian, 30; stress hormones released by, 54, 70–71, 93, 94, 100, 113, 129, 161–62 (*see also* stress hormones)

anxiety, 188; catastrophic thinking
and, 142–43; misunderstanding
of mechanisms underlying,
189–90; panic vs., 81–82, 179–80;
from personal relationships,
184; social, 181–82; treatment
model for, 180–84, 190
arousal, 127; alarm/danger/fear
conflated with, 58–59; amygdala and, 58; defined, 5; fear
and, 54–55; as normal, 49–55;
sympathetic nervous system
and, 28. *See also* hyperarousal
arousal regulation: automatic, 153;
CBT and, 5–6; child-caregiver
relationship and, 28–30, 33–34,
49–55; evolution of, 30–31;
relationship and, 32–33, 79; unconscious procedural memory
and, 185
arousal regulation systems:
alarm attenuation and, 121–22;
autonomic nervous system
and, 19–21; evolution of, 30–31,
87; executive function, 69–71;
hierarchy of, 67, 75–79, 87,
121–22, 190; immobilization
system, 67–68; internal replica
system, 71–74; mobilization
system, 69; relationship and,
79; social engagement system,
71; underdevelopment of,
89. *See also* immobilization
system; internal replica system;
mobilization system; social
engagement system
autonomic nervous system, 19–21,

180, 191. *See also* parasympathetic nervous system; sympathetic nervous system
awareness, inner, 143–47, 149–50

babies, 50, 53, 105, 106–7
Bateman, Anthony, 33
Beebe, Beatrice, 52, 53
body awareness, 145–46
body language, 125, 192
Botox, 28
Bowlby, John, 33
brain: alarm system of, 109; stress
hormones needed for, 81; unconscious procedural memory
in, 12–13; visual processing center of, 166. *See also* amygdala;
cortex; subcortex; *specific part*
breastfeeding, 45
breathing exercises, 4, 5
bridges: fear of, 9, 176, 188–89;
safety of, 162; Ten-Day Plan for,
176–78
Bruce Banner (cartoon character), 104, 106–7

calming person: Alarm Attenuation Exercise involving, 129–31;
anxiety control and, 183; memories of, 35–36, 105–7, 125–26,
160, 192–93; parasympathetic
nervous system activation and,
180–81, 183; photographs of,
130, 160; stressful situations
linked to, 153, 162, 167, 181; therapist as, 157–58; Three-Button

activation of, 71; defined, 28; up-regulation by, 19–20, 192

Ten-Day Plan: for bridge crossings, 176–78; FAQs, 157–60; general instructions, 100, 153–56; linking exercise, 157–60; for MRIs, 163–66; for tunnel passages, 172–75; for visits to high places, 168–72
Tenerife (Canary Islands) airline crash (1977), 113
tension, 98, 103–4
thoughts: control of, 4–5; negative, 142–43; out-of-control, 82; redirection of, 7–8; stopping, 7; "what if" thoughts, 164–65, 171, 174, 177–78
Three-Button Exercise, 126–29, 156
tickling, 51–52
time, sense of, 105
touch: alarm attenuation and, 129–31; calming signals in, 123, 125; child-caregiver relationship and, 23–24, 28; child's expectations of, 110; memories of, 28, 36, 94–95; oxytocin-producing links established with, 105–7; parasympathetic nervous system activated by, 23–24, 95; reexperiencing of, 192; stressful situations linked to, 39, 94–95, 153, 154–55, 181, 183; vagal-braking links established with, 101–5
training, 185

trauma, 59, 117–18
trust, 57, 92
tunnels: fear of, 9, 17–19, 24–25, 36, 37, 98, 172, 188–89; safety of, 162; Ten-Day Plan for, 172–75
turbulence, in-flight, 18

unconditional positive regard, 32–33, 34
unconscious procedural memory: arousal regulation and, 185; panic/claustrophobia controlled with, 49; parasympathetic nervous system and, 23–24, 28–29, 94–95; pilot experiences using, 111–12; programming of, 159; stress hormones and, 12–13, 44, 94–95; during Ten-Day Plan, 159–60; training of, 20–21
University of California, San Diego, 146
University of Connecticut School of Medicine, 59
University of Illinois, Chicago, 193
University of North Carolina, 193
University of Texas, Austin, 51

vagal braking: activation of, 72, 110, 180, 183; anxiety control through, 183; child-caregiver relationship and, 49–50; defined, 20, 32; evolution of, 191; link establishment, 100–105; panic/claustrophobia prevented with, 37–41, 44, 45,

About the Author

Captain Tom Bunn, MSW, LCSW, became a leading authority on panic disorder during his former career as an airline pilot. After graduating from Wake Forest University in psychology, Captain Tom entered the US Air Force. Number one in his aviation cadet class when he got his wings, he was given his choice of assignments and chose to fly the Air Force's first supersonic jet fighter, the F-100. After leaving the Air Force, he joined Pan Am, where he volunteered to work in the airline's fear-of-flying course. Many course participants were afraid to fly because of panic attacks.

He is the founder of SOAR Inc., which provides treatment for in-flight panic sufferers, and the author of *SOAR: The Breakthrough Treatment for Fear of Flying*. Bunn is a regular contributor to *Psychology Today*, and his work has been featured in the *New York Times*, the *Boston Globe*, *Newsweek* (cover story), *Time*, the *Wall Street Journal*, *USA Today*, and many other publications. He has appeared on ABC's *Good Morning America*, *Regis*, CNN, Fox, and MSNBC and contributed a chapter to *Clinical Applications of the Polyvagal Theory: The Emergence of Polyvagal-Informed Therapies*, edited by Stephen W. Porges and Deb A. Dana. He lives in Connecticut with his wife, Marie.

For more information, visit www.fearofflying.com or www.panicfree.net.